THE
ATTITUDE
CHECK

Laura,

Thank you for your
leadership!

THE ATTITUDE CHECK

Lessons in Leadership

HEATH SUDDLESON

TATE PUBLISHING
AND ENTERPRISES, LLC

Published by Tate Publishing & Enterprises, LLC
127 E. Trade Center Terrace | Mustang, Oklahoma 73064 USA
1.888.361.9473 | www.tatepublishing.com

Tate Publishing is committed to excellence in the publishing industry. The company reflects the philosophy established by the founders, based on Psalm 68:11,
"The Lord gave the word and great was the company of those who published it."

Book design copyright © 2013 by Tate Publishing, LLC. All rights reserved.
Cover design by Jan Sunday Quilaquil
Interior design by Jake Muelle

Published in the United States of America

ISBN: 978-1-62563-583-9
1. Business & Economics / Leadership
2. Business & Economics / Management
13.04.01

TABLE OF CONTENTS

INTRODUCTION

"These lessons don't apply only to business, Joe. A genuinely sound business principle will apply anywhere in life—in your friendships, in your marriage, *anywhere*. That's the true bottom line. Not whether it simply improves your financial balance sheet, but whether it improves your *life's* balance sheet."

—Bob Burg and John David Mann, *The Go-Giver*

Welcome to a journey on leadership. On this journey, we will explore various types of leadership, what makes leadership effective, and how to choose the path to becoming the leader we want to be. That long journey begins with a single diagnostic, an attitude check.

This is important because companies are not looking for managers. Companies are looking for leaders. Management is a task-oriented activity—meaning that we manage projects or tasks, but we lead people. Someone who has both skill sets of management and leadership can accomplish great things. Unfortunately, companies are more willing to teach management skills than they are willing to teach leadership skills. They want you to do that work on your own, or come to the table with those skills already. Yet between the two skills of management and leadership, it is the leadership that is perhaps the more important skill. As Zig Ziglar once said, "Your attitude, not your aptitude, will determine your altitude."

If you ever examine a dysfunctional team and interview the team members to see what they think needs to change, they will rarely suggest that they need management. What they beg for is leadership. People at their core crave the structure, process, and respect that come with great leadership.

Perhaps the most common mistake made among leaders is not doing an attitude check early and often. This is not about the attitude of your subordinates but, rather, your own. It is much easier to control your own attitude than it is to control the attitudes of others. Luckily, controlling your own attitude can often have great influence over the attitudes of others, by creating the environment that then allows them to change their own. The first attitude we need to set is that you need them much more than they need you. Imagine trying to perform every task specific to each aspect of your organization by yourself. You can't do it. You need them.

Sure, you might be thinking that you can easily replace each one of them if it came to that. Maybe you can, but at what cost? Just in terms of the time and resources it takes to find and train someone, replacement of staff should be your last option. There is also a serious morale issue when you have a high-turnover environment. People are spending almost as much time searching for their next position as they are working for you simply because they don't know if they will have a job next week.

There are two basic types of leadership we need to clarify here. The first is *command and control*. This is the type of leadership you might find in many military environments. You bark orders, and your subordinates will obey them with perfect precision. This sounds good in theory, but it requires much more time on your part to lead your troops than if you took a much different approach. This type of leadership requires an inordinate amount of time for training, which is more than what most companies and other organizations have available. Remember that the military begins with some form of recruit training or boot camp that lasts no less than a couple of months. From there the training continues in specialized schools, which can also take months. This is all before a new team member ever arrives on the job.

Another reason that this style works well in the military is because there are many who want that military structure and mentality. People who volunteer to serve in the armed forces are particularly geared to this type of treatment. In my case, I enlisted in the United States Marine Corps specifically because I wanted a greater challenge than I felt the other services could offer. In the normal workplace there are some who will respond well to this type of environment, however, the greater majority will not respond as well. More importantly, for most who would respond well to the command and control format, they also respond well to the second leadership model.

This is also the type of leadership that typically uses the employee's paycheck as leverage to get more productivity. While that may work for a short time, you will never get long-term dedication from your staff because you have made the paycheck the most important characteristic of their job, and every company offers a paycheck.

The second type of leadership is *responsibility and reward*. The premise of this is extremely obvious, yet rarely implemented. You simply give your subordinates some specified responsibility and then reward them for a job well done.

Your attitude check should first determine which type of leader you wish to be. Do you want to simply bark orders and have them followed with military precision, or do you want to develop your staff so that they can do more, thus freeing you to focus on other aspects of your organization? Imagine how much time is wasted when leaders have to bark endless orders, unable to leave their staff alone with their daily tasks.

This is actually micromanaging. When managers micromanage their team, so much time and effort is spent on essentially two people doing the same task. Leaders do not micromanage. Leaders empower their teams and let them work. Micromanagers are focused on their own goals and outcomes. Leaders are there to serve. Whether they are serving in a volunteer organization or serving their company in a leadership role, leaders work best when the focus is not on their own goals and outcomes but on those whom they serve.

We learn about the leaders we want to be by watching those who inspire us, and we learn a lot about the leaders we don't want to be by working under the command of leaders who deflate us. When searching for your own leadership style, try to balance the lessons you've learned from those leaders you like with those from leaders you didn't like. Sometimes we have a tendency to go in totally the opposite direction of the leader we don't like. It's better to observe a healthy balance.

Consider that while you are working to answer this question, "What type of leader you want to be?", you will need to practice some of these tactics in real life situations. During this stage, exploring your leadership style is much like trying on a new suit or dress. What looked good on one person might not suit you as well. It just doesn't fit your style and personality. Not a problem. Simply try on another style and keep trying on different styles until you find the one that fits. Once you have found the style that fits, you can then accessorize your new outfit by honing skills more specific to what you need for further development.

The second part of your attitude check is to focus on who your customer really is. If you are a leader in a volunteer organization, you need to realize that the other volunteers are your customers. Even if you are supervising them, they are the folks you need to take care of first. This is called *servant leadership*. If you are dealing with a paid staff in a business environment, you have several levels of customers. They include outside clients, or end users of your products, as well as other departments; even your employees are still your customers. You probably understand that in tighter job markets, you need to work to attract the right candidates and hire your staff wisely. Well, sometimes you need to work just as hard to keep them. If you have done a good job with responsibility and reward, you might not even have to increase salaries to keep talented staff because you have made the environment worth more than the paycheck. This is not to imply that you don't need to pay staff fairly. You do. This is simply recognition of the fact that if you have built the right environment, it will take more than a small pay raise for someone to convince your team member to switch teams. Without building this rewarding environment, your team members might already be searching for a reason to leave and that 1% pay increase might just do the trick. I have even seen staff leave to take another position for less money because the environment was so bad that even the salary was not a motivating factor.

Another critical aspect to customers is that regardless of the position, there is always an element of customer service. Because someone relies on the service we are performing, we have a customer. Even if the person we are dealing with at any moment is not a customer in the true sense of the word, we need to go beyond *customer service* and offer *human service*. When we focus on customer service, we focus on that person purchasing our product or service either for the first time or as a repeat customer. When we focus on human service we focus on that person's human needs for recognition, validation, and respect. You will never go wrong treating your customers and/or team members as humans.

The third part of your attitude check is to focus on the goals. The idea here is to look for function and not fanfare. If your mission is wrapped more in protocol than it is in performance, then perhaps you have missed your target. In the military, personnel snap to attention when a senior officer enters the room, unless they are engaged in critical work functions. Even the military recognizes that the mission trumps fanfare. What do you expect from your employees? Do you expect fanfare, which makes you unapproachable, or do you expect results in a manner that encourages every employee to offer ideas of ways to improve your organization?

Let's put this in today's business terms. Imagine that some young apprentice has figured out a way to do something faster and with lower costs. Meanwhile, you have already spent thousands of dollars on equipment to get you to where you already were. As hard as it may seem to believe now, some managers would stifle new ideas in order to justify the cost of a recently employed system. Remember that innovation knows no rank. The best ideas for how to improve processes are much more likely to come from the low-level person who has to do the same task day after day and complains to team mates about how much easier it would be if... Your attitude will be the difference between that low-level team member feeling safe to approach you with a new idea or that person simply keeping quiet to maintain the status quo.

I have heard many executives say they have an open-door policy, yet they have a gauntlet of gatekeepers who make it very difficult for staff to stop by and share ideas. I worked for one company that not only had a "mahogany row" where all the executives sat together, but there was also a badge access point to enter this area even though the point of entry was already in the secure office space. This was a very clear barrier that contradicted any declaration of an open-door policy.

Some of the best executives I have worked with made it a point to walk around the office periodically and speak to the employees. They would stop by each desk and have a short conversation with each staff member. This might have been done once each month or once each quarter, depending on how large the organization. I worked for a company called Daniel, Mann, Johnson, and Mendenhall, which had over thirty thousand employees in offices all over the world. Even with a company that large, the president would visit the offices and make it a point to walk the office floor. It might be six months or a year between visits, but those visits went a long way to helping everyone feel connected to the company leadership. Company newsletter messages and appearances at large gatherings are nice, but they do not provide the value gained from personal connections.

Okay, so you've read about the parts of the attitude checks, and I'll bet right now you're still thinking that they need you more than you need them because you are the one with all the historical knowledge of the organization, and without you as a resource, they can't do their jobs. You're probably right, but they can do another job for another person. They really don't need you that badly—unless you are a great leader. In the chapters that follow, we will discuss the key aspects of leadership and the attitudes that will carry you to success.

Try to remember overall that as a leader, you need to do two very simple things. The first is to empower your team. Let them know what their job is, and let them know that they have your permission to do it. This may sound like a concept that is so elementary you are now wondering what you will gain from this book, but consider this: many managers fail because they assign tasks and then sabotage the effort before the subordinate has had the opportunity to complete the assigned task. When you empower your team, you back off and let them work. In later chapters, we will explore the ways that managers sabotage the effort of their team.

The second critical thing to do is to enable your team. This simply means that you provide the necessary tools and remove obstacles from their paths. These obstacles may be difficult work processes or challenges in personnel. When your team feels that they have been empowered and enabled, there is no limit to what they can accomplish. You can empower and enable your team with your attitude.

The key is to remember that no leader wants to fail, or be demeaning to his or her team. Quite the opposite. Most leaders who fail do so because they don't inspire out of their teams the production that is needed to sustain the organization. Most leaders who are harsh are not trying to be harsh, but they are so worried about doing a good job overall that they forget to remember key people skills or attitude checks.

- ✓ You need your team more than they need you.
- ✓ What type of leader do you want to be?
- ✓ Who are your customers?
- ✓ Whose goals are you focused on?
- ✓ Are you approachable?
- ✓ Are you empowering and enabling your team?

DOING WHAT YOU LOVE

"Whatever you are, be a good one."
—Abraham Lincoln

The very first attitude check in this chapter has to be a self-diagnostic. Do you love what you are doing? And are you doing what you love? No, this is not the same question asked two ways. They are entirely different perspectives and may yield two entirely different answers.

When I speak to high school students, I always tell them that it is important to go to college and get a degree in something. The most important thing is for them to pursue a degree in something that they love. The reason is simple. If you love what you are doing, and if you are doing what you love, then you will put more energy and effort into your endeavors. In short, that energy and effort combine to become passion. With more passion, you will demonstrate exceptional skill and experience exceptional results. It follows that if you do something exceptionally well, then the money will follow.

What course of study people get their degree in is not usually as important as the fact that they have one. Sure, for some types of work, it is important to have a degree in a particular field of study. It is difficult to imagine biochemical research being performed by someone with a liberal arts degree, and certainly, engineering requires a level of knowledge gained through classes in engineering. Still, for a large majority of professions, your degree represents a portable set of skills and abilities. Many people find work in a field in which they are not degreed only to accumulate enough work experience, or they pursue a master's degree in that specific field later to propel them forward. Those who do this are probably doing so because they have discovered that they are now doing what they love.

Let's take a look at the first question in this chapter. Do you love what you are doing? Even though you may be in a field that you love, you might find that the tasks you are performing or the organization for whom you are working are not what you love. You are close, but not quite there. You need to take stock of what you love about your field and then examine that against why you do not love what you are doing.

The second question may seem at first like the obvious extension of the previous question, but it is not. You may love what you are doing, but you may also love something else more. If you can identify something that beckons you more than what you are currently doing, then you are not doing what you love.

The best example I can give of this duality are the circumstances surrounding the writing of this book. I have been working in construction management for more than twenty-five years, and I have loved doing it. I have never had the same day twice, working on many different types of projects has been an incredible journey; and best of all, I can go to any of the projects that I have worked on and see that I have had a hand at building something that serves so many people. Still, what I would love to be doing even more is writing this book and speaking to people about leadership and the lessons that I have learned along my own journey. I realize that I have a greater love that has compelled me to write this book. I could not have known twenty-five years ago that this would eventually be my path. I had to choose something that was available to me at the time, based on the skill sets that I possessed at that time.

Only after I have had opportunities to lead others in many different roles, and with many different outcomes, did I realize what I had to offer through this new path. The key lesson here is that what you loved yesterday may not be what you love today. You might even love what you are doing, but you are not doing what you love because there is something else out there that beckons you more.

With this new perspective, let's ask those questions again. This time, let us explore the answers a bit more.

Do you love what you are doing? When you go to work every day, are you happy about the day ahead, or are you searching for any reason to turn around? If you are taking a lot of unscheduled personal days, if you are not looking forward to the day ahead, if you are consistently showing up late to work, if you are not feeling that you are living up to your potential, then there is something critical in your job that you do not love. Yes, it is that straightforward. The good news is that once you have identified the issue, you can work to address it. And there are many different ways to get back on track.

Of course, just realizing that you do not love what you are doing is not the end of the process. You need to determine where the disconnect has occurred. Are there certain tasks that you do not enjoy that have begun to dominate your time? Are there people you work with that make your job difficult? Have the tasks you are performing become so repetitive that you are no longer being intellectually challenged or stimulated? It may be helpful to you to do a personality assessment such as DISC or Myers-Briggs if you have not done so already.

For my own personality, I find that I am much more productive when I am doing something that excites me. I am a strong D in DISC, and I love coming into a troubled situation, assessing the various factors, and working to find resolutions to conflicts. In the construction industry, this often gives me the opportunity to make judgment recommendations. What I do not enjoy is the repetitive data entry that comes with some project management software applications that are necessary for me to illustrate my findings. I don't mind using the word-processing software to write hundreds of pages of text because it was the outpouring of my time and talents. It is the slow, simple, arduous, and excruciatingly repetitive task of entering raw data into various database fields that causes me the most agony. Let me be clear. It is not the software but my intolerance of the data entry process. In fact, I have no trouble training staff on how to use the software, or speaking about the functions of the software at professional conferences. I actually enjoy those aspects of the software. It is my own shortcoming that I have no interest in performing this data entry because I had done it for more than twenty years. The data entry process has lost all of its appeal to me. It was my own attitude that I needed to check, but until I understood the disconnect, I was unable to resolve the problem.

One other key attitude check to determine whether you are doing what you love and loving what you are doing is whether or not you are afraid to move forward. It is possible to do what you love, and love what you are doing, but still be reluctant to take the next steps forward. Sometimes it is a matter of the security of knowing your current role and being in your comfort zone. Sometimes it is the fear of not doing well at the next level. Sometimes it is just a time constraint and the feeling that we don't have enough time now. If we are struggling with time management now, how will we manage with more responsibility?

We will always find time to do those things that captivate us. When faced with several tasks at once, are you not more likely to begin the task that excites you more? This is one of the reasons that people lose so much time on social media and other websites, because they have found something that has captivated them and drawn their interest. Who knew pictures of cats could be so enjoyable?

Another crucial attitude check is to determine whether we are being a leader who is embracing the opportunity to take on the next role, or if we are being a reluctant leader who is taking on the role only after having an arm or two twisted before accepting the challenge.

I learned this lesson in Toastmasters. In my first three years of leadership service above the level of my own club, I had been the reluctant leader. There were three roles that I accepted: area governor, division governor, and then lieutenant governor of marketing at the district level—all of which I had taken reluctantly. In all three of those cases, I learned some lessons, and even enjoyed myself; but my lessons were limited because my attitude was one of indifference. In fact, for the latter two positions, I had to interview with a nomination committee; and in both of those interviews, I would not have been at all upset if the committee had not nominated me for the positions.

When I accepted the role of lieutenant governor of marketing, I had made the commitment to fill all fours roles in that track. Those were lieutenant governor of marketing, lieutenant governor of education and training, district governor, and immediate past district governor, and each position would last one year. Because I had taken the first role with the expectation and commitment of taking all four roles, I went to the nomination committee with an entirely different attitude when I interviewed for lieutenant governor of education and training. This time, I was excited about the possibilities that lay ahead, and I had real plans for what I would accomplish once I assumed the role.

It was in moving from a reluctant attitude to an embracing attitude that I recognized that for the first time in my leadership development I realized how much I was holding myself back. I was now better able to recognize some of my own shortcomings. I discovered a profound difference in my openness to learn, grow, and develop once I started looking forward to the next steps. It was at this time that I realized how I loved what I was doing, and that I was doing what I loved. It was during this time I realized that I had a passion that could be harnessed.

- ✓ Do you love what you are doing?
- ✓ Are you doing what you love?
- ✓ Are you afraid to move forward?
- ✓ Are you reluctant to lead?
- ✓ Are you embracing opportunities?

BUILDING YOUR TEAM

"Talent wins games, but teamwork and intelligence wins championships."

—Michael Jordan

The team is the core of what leadership is all about. If we could just do everything ourselves, we wouldn't need to worry about whether or not we are effective as leaders. Since we can't do everything ourselves, and since harnessing the power of a team allows us to achieve greater feats than we could do by ourselves, we need to surround ourselves with a team.

No one can know everything. No one expects you to know everything. The key is to surround yourself with a variety of people. You need some people who know more than you so that you can keep learning and developing, and you need some people who know less than you so that you can train and mentor others. Mentors should be a significant part of your team structure, even if they are outside your day-to-day operation. I have seen some companies that have an established mentorship program where mentees are assigned their mentors. While I applaud the efforts to have an organized mentorship program, I find that mentorships are a personal relationship that will be better utilized if mentees can choose their own mentors. A simple analogy is that while I have a lot of neckties hanging in my closet, I find the ones I wear are the ones I chose myself.

Whether you are building your team for the first time, inheriting someone else's team, or simply examining the efficiency of your current team, you must start with what structure you are looking to use. We have all heard of an Organizational Chart, but I encourage you to think of yours as an Accountability Structure. After all, isn't that what you really want from your team? By focusing on where the different points of accountability will be in your team, you will have an easier time building one.

Sometimes you get to select your team members, and sometimes you don't. That's life, and nothing I write can change that. Sorry. But in understanding that, we will deal with both situations.

In the case of selecting your own team members, the first bit of advice I can give you is to avoid the trust trap. This is where we scrutinize candidates during the selection process, interview them two or three times, have other colleagues interview them to verify our observations, hire them, and then fail to trust them. The first part of this trap is what we are supposed to be doing. We should be scrutinizing candidates, interviewing them, and having our observations verified. So with all of the effort and analysis we have invested in them, why do we fail to trust them to do what we selected them to do? This is one way that we begin to sabotage our own efforts when we watch them like hawks, criticize their work, and do many other things to make them feel that they are not valued members of the team. For those of you who have great difficulty in trusting others, consider that you need to trust yourself. This is to say that if you have done a good job on the selection of your team member, then you can rest assured that the person you selected is the right choice and you can let them work.

I once worked for a company that used the term *organ rejection* to explain why some people came to the company in the middle of their careers but could not assimilate to this company's way of doing things. Managers would simply say, "Bob is no longer with the company. It was another case of organ rejection."

I was a mid-career hire myself and began to realize that organ rejection was the perfect analogy for this issue, but not because of how the term was used. In fact, it was entirely the opposite interpretation. When organ rejection occurs in the human body, it is not the organ rejecting the host. It is the host body rejecting the organ. Even though this organ has been medically tested to be a good match, and even though doctors have certified that the organ is in good working order, the host body has trouble accepting this new team member. So, too, did it work with our company. We had reviewed their resumes to type-test the candidate to the company. We interviewed them and had several managers sign off on how the candidate appeared to be in good working order, but then when it came time to work with them, the company had a difficult time interacting with this new team member.

Rather than harnessing the diverse experience of this team member, and rather than looking for ways to make the transition to our company culture more understandable, we would often stifle the talent that we had acquired and end up deflating someone who could have made some significant contributions. This brings about another attitude check. Are you working to accept or reject a transplanted organ?

Presuming that you have brought on a new team member, and that you have not rejected this new organ, there will be a period of time that this person is new on your team, and you may not want them to make command decisions. It will only help you to have this discussion with them and encourage them to consult you on key decisions until you have a better feel for their level of judgment. After that "breaking-in" period, you need to stop being a control freak and let them do the job that you selected them to do. If you had the time to do their job yourself, you wouldn't have needed to bring them into your team in the first place.

Some people, when selecting their team, will choose people because of friendships rather than capabilities. I have seen this happen most in politics and in volunteer organizations, but I have seen this happen in the private sector as well. While this friendship trap may not be as common as the trust trap, it has the potential to be far more destructive. If the friend you have chosen has the skill set to do the work, and do it well, then things could go very well. It can still be problematic because friends often have a difficult time confronting each other when things are not going well. This obstacle to communication goes both ways. Sometimes supervisors have an aversion to confronting a friend who is not performing well, and sometimes a team member has an aversion to confronting a friend who is not leading well.

If, however, your friend does not have the skill set necessary to do the job well, then others around will become less motivated because it will be obvious to them that friendships are more important to you than the job at hand. Other team members might also become resentful if they feel they have to accommodate extra workload that your friend cannot deal with. You also run the risk of losing the friendship if you try to get your friend to improve his performance. You have to do an attitude check to determine if you are in business to hire friends and whether or not you put function above friendship.

I once worked for a company where a friend of the department manager's was trying to get his daughter a job. The department manager was all too happy to hire her and do his friend a favor. The problem was that she was not really interested in this line of work, though she was happy to receive the paycheck. The position had been open because there was so much to be done, but instead of her helping with the workload, all the other team members had to pick up the extra slack. Although she had the talent to do the work, she lacked the passion and motivation. In the end, she did not perform well on the job, and it demoralized the entire team.

The traits you would want to look for in an addition to your team are dependability, integrity, initiative, and contentment. I will discuss each of these in order.

Dependability is just what it implies. You want someone who is going to be there day in and day out. You want to have someone whom you can find or contact. This also means that they follow through on tasks assigned to them with little or no follow-up. You will find plenty of people who work very well when micromanaged. If you give them a simple task, they will complete it and be right back at your desk for the next assignment. These people need a lot of hand-holding, and you don't need to spend that kind of time. You want someone whom you can give a series of tasks and they complete them all. It is even better if you can find someone whom you can simply tell the desired result and they will figure out the tasks on their own.

Integrity is also pretty obvious, but sometimes it's hard to be sure. People can talk a good game, but when it's time to perform, you find the real person you selected for the job. Someone with integrity will make sure that they are adding value to your organization. They will not make excuses when things go wrong, and they will choose to tell you what you need to hear instead of what they think you want to hear. Integrity is what helps them deal honestly with other team members when you are not around.

Though it's not always possible to do so, I like to play golf with people before I do business with them. The reason is that I will find out everything I need to know about them in just four hours on the golf course. For example, if they score a 7 on a hole but put a 6 on the scorecard, I know that this is a person who cannot be trusted. If they are going to lie about a simple and fun game, what will they lie about when money or reputations are on the line? I will also find out how well they deal with adversity. Every golfer hits an errant shot every now and then—okay, some more than others. Does the person get visibly upset and angry, or do they take it in stride? My golf game is not good. I will own that now. My handicap is the game of golf, but I enjoy the challenge and the opportunity to socialize. I once had a friend, who was a golf pro, tell me that he preferred playing with me than some other golfers who were much better golfers. He told me it was because I had fun even though the game took longer to play. Because I had fun, so did he.

Another thing you will find out on the golf course is whether the person has a tendency to use inappropriate comments or humor. Many jokes are told on the golf course, and many one-liners about the quality of one's game are thrown out for good measure. You will know quickly whether this person will get along with you and the other members of the team. I also like to watch to see how they treat the staff at the course. Do they tip the beverage cart driver and say thank you? These are basic ways to show recognition and will translate into how they treat other members of your team. Are they kind to staff at the golf course, or do they get short tempered and impatient? Do they treat the staff as though they feel superior? These are all danger signs to watch out for. Some of these traits can be observed in places other than the golf course, but if you ever wondered why so much business was conducted on the golf course, now you know.

Initiative is a key trait for anyone on my team. I want my team members always thinking of everything that needs to be done. I have enough to do with my own job responsibilities I don't need to constantly be worried about theirs. I am filling the position because I need someone to do this for me, not because I want to double my workload to get the job done. Look for someone who is a self-starter and is always looking for more to do. The best byproduct of initiative is innovation, and as I said before, innovation knows no rank. Some of the most junior members of the team will come up with some fantastic ways to improve your work processes. Be open to their suggestions.

The last trait to look for is contentment. This refers to the person's personality. Do they seem generally happy in life, or are they always complaining about something? If this is someone who is always complaining, they will be a constant distraction to your mission and goals. This does not mean that complaints are never valid or warranted, but rather, it's a judgment you need to make about how much time and energy this person will take. Even if you think this person is ethical and talented, if they are a constant complainer, they will be a constant obstacle to your success. A contented person is not only one less thing to worry about in terms of you receiving unexpected resignations, but a contented person can also be a stabilizing force in your team when others might be dealing with issues of discontent.

You might be thinking that you know how to handle a discontented or complaining person. You might even be thinking that you can help this person change. No, you can't, and no, you can't. You also are not thinking about all your other team members who will have difficulty dealing with this person. Your best course of action is to avoid this person and find a better team member.

No assessment is complete without evaluating your team members' strengths and weaknesses. Try to find people whose strengths will make their doing the job easy, and maybe even fun. If someone is not an organized person, asking them to keep your files is not a wise choice. You might even need to reorganize job responsibilities to accommodate team members' strengths and weaknesses.

Try to find the solution that has everyone doing what they do well. Have the attitude that you want to play to people's strengths.

Diversity in your team is more important than some people realize. You may not even be aware if you are selecting team members from a single group of people that does not end up representative of your organization. This does not mean that you need to select people based solely on diversity, but you better believe that people will take notice whether you intended to be exclusive or not. Also, remember that with greater diversity comes greater field of vision. The more perspectives you have on your team, the better you will be able to cater to more markets.

Clearly, building your own team needs to be something that is given the proper amount of time and consideration. It may be better to leave some positions unfilled until the right candidate can be found rather just a person whose best quality is being 98.6 degrees. You will do more damage to your team if this person is unproductive, or even worse, a destructive member on the team. Your attitude should be one of protecting your team.

Though not having much input into a team's development might be frustrating at times, some of my greatest lessons in leadership come from having to work with people I did not select myself. They were assigned to you, or they were already there, or they might even have been elected to the position. In any case, you are going to need to work with them. In this situation, building your team is not the act of filling the positions but, rather, the act of establishing structure, improving performance, and resolving issues.

In some cases, it is your first-time meeting, so you can take the opportunity to set some ground rules. I had an excellent case of this when my team was working on a new building at Radford University. I was the construction manager for the architect, and I was just meeting the general contractor's team. This is a traditionally adversarial relationship, and I had just come off of a project where the relationship between my company and the general contractor was damaged beyond repair. Not wanting to repeat the stress and angst of the last project, I had a talk with this new general contractor's team. We agreed to try to work together to help each other succeed. We acknowledged that each party was there to make money, but not through unethical practices; and we agreed that we would work to support each other rather than look for opportunities to point fingers and posture for claims later on. It worked so well that we finished the project early and on budget, and each company made money. Even the owner was happy at the end of the project.

If you have met before, there might be disagreements or conflicts, which you are bringing with you like the proverbial baggage. My sincere advice here is to take it head-on. Have a private meeting with the person and put the facts on the table.

Fact 1 You both have a job to do, and you rely on the other person to get it done.

Fact 2 These issues between you exist, and that may not change.

Fact 3 You need to make an agreement on how you will work together, and communicate with each other. Call it a *working contract*.

You want to make sure this working contract covers all the basics of how often you will meet, your preferred ways to communicate with each other, acceptable time frames for responses, limits of authority, and methods to resolve disputes.

For example, one person may prefer to communicate via e-mail while the other prefers phone conversations. One person may prefer to involve a manager to help resolve disputes, while the other person might prefer to try to resolve disputes between yourselves.

Once you have done this, you can have discussions about the facts. Try to avoid accusatory statements or tones. Statements that bring emotion to the forefront will not help you focus on the facts. These statements will instead drive you farther away from any amicable resolution. Here are some quick examples:

Instead of: "You wouldn't cooperate with me before, and that needs to change."

Try: "We didn't work well together, but perhaps now we can."

Instead of: "You never returned my calls, and that doesn't work for me."

Try: "Do you prefer to communicate by phone, e-mail, or some other method?"

Anytime you can avoid putting someone on the defensive to start, you have a much greater chance of success in identifying the issues and the solutions. The use of "we" statements instead of "I" or "you" statements conveys a team approach rather than an attacking posture. Also work to avoid the word *but* in your responses to your team member. Even when you say "Yes, okay" or "Fine," your teammate will not have heard the acceptance and will react to the negation of their last statement. Substitute the word *and* instead.

What was "I prefer to communicate over the phone" answered by "Okay, but we need to document our conversations and agreements" becomes "Yes, and we need to find a way to document our conversations and agreements."

You might want to find a neutral place to meet. Perhaps a nice restaurant where you can share a meal will provide a good setting to negotiate your truce and cease-fire. Notice I did not say "your surrender," or even "their surrender." You may not be able to resolve whatever issues are causing conflict. If you can, that's great, but be fully prepared to leave the issues in place. Your goal here is to find ways to work around them. For example, let's take a situation where the person you are working with has a history of making agreements or commitments and then later claiming the agreements or commitments were not as you describe. You are not going to change their behavior, but you can put forth in your working contract that you want all agreements in writing. This won't necessarily make them suddenly honor their commitments, but at least you can verify your understanding with the written agreements. The best tool in this agreement is an attitude of partnership versus having an adversarial approach.

There is one last aspect to team building that should be recognized here. It's the aspect of growth and transition. How do you get your organization from point C to point D? You have successfully passed points A and B, and now you are ready to take your organization farther to accomplish some great things. The reality is that some of the team members who helped you get where you are now may not be the right team members to take you to the next level. We have a tendency to want to be loyal to those who have been there for us, and these may even be long-term team members. This does not change the fact that they may not possess the skill set or the attitude that we need to move forward.

Once you have recognized that you need to make a staff change, it is important to show appreciation for the person who has helped you get this far. This is not just for the sake of the person whose role in the team is changing or ending, but it is also important for the rest of the team members to see that you do care about them. They see the way you treat one employee as the way that you will treat them too.

The best way to manage the transitional team process is to first set very clear expectations about where your organization is going and how you are going to get there. What do you need from each team member? How is this different from the way you have been doing things? The second thing is to show appreciation for all team members who have gotten you to this point and sympathize with the fact that the process of change is not always easy. Have a set time frame of how long you will give them to make the adaptation to the new process before you begin to make changes in the team. Then step back and give your team the room to change their pace. There are some who will realize that this new direction is not for them, and they will remove themselves from the team. Some others may need to be told it's time to go. Again, just because they helped you get to where you are does not mean that they are the right person to take you farther. They deserve your appreciation, and even your loyalty, but not at the expense of the future of your organization. Too often, that loyalty forces us to keep the person in the position that prevents us from moving forward. We may be great where we are, but we cannot get better either. Having an attitude of having the right team to move forward will make all the difference.

All teams, regardless of whether the members have been selected or supplied, need a clear structure to operate. When people are clear on their role and the roles of others, things move much more smoothly. Most problems can be avoided by having clearly defined roles and responsibilities. Then maintain the organizational structure until you have evidence that something is not working and should be changed.

- ✓ Are you working to avoid organ rejection?
- ✓ Are you in business to hire friends?
- ✓ Do you put function above friendship?
- ✓ Do you play to people's strengths?
- ✓ Are you protecting your team?
- ✓ Are you working for partnership or are you adversarial?
- ✓ Do you have the right team to move forward?

HAVING CLEAR EXPECTATIONS AND A BUY-IN

"The Secret Formula is not an organizational chart; it is a map to clarify the roles and relationships within an effective organization."

—Jim Brown, *The Imperfect Board Member*

You can see exactly what you want it to look like. You know exactly how this is going to work. Every step and every detail is clear in your mind, so why doesn't the end product come out the way you expected?

One of the most common problems in organizations is when the leader and the subordinates do not have a clear and mutual understanding of what is expected. Another is that while expectations are clear, they are not agreed to. Simply proclaiming that something needs to be done is not enough. You need to get the buy-in of your team because too many people will pick the highway over your way.

Very often, failures in the team are actually failures of communicating expectations clearly. You had a clear idea of what you expected this person to do when you brought them on board, but they did not have the same expectations.

Perhaps they anticipated it would take less effort, or that the rewards would be greater, but there was not a clear understanding between the two parties. Without knowing the specifics of each case, you cannot assess who was not clear; but suffice it to say that in any agreement, each party is responsible for making sure things are very clear. This may take some type of written agreement; however, whether your agreement is written or verbal, your attitude should be one of understanding that misunderstandings will still happen. Do your best to be clear, and do your best to be patient when misunderstandings occur.

The first step in making sure that your team member understands the situation is to ask them to paraphrase, or even repeat, the assignment back to you. This may seem childish at first, but I assure you that one of three things will happen.

Possible outcome number 1 is that what you hear back is a wonderful summation of the task at hand. In fact you might be thinking that you could not have said it better yourself.

Possible outcome number 2 is that what you hear back is similar to, but not exactly, what you were certain you conveyed. Perhaps there were some details missing, or perhaps they added in some expectations that did not match. In either case, this will cause you to start the communication over again to ensure that you are on a common wavelength.

Possible outcome number 3 is that what you hear back does not sound at all like what you conveyed, because they paraphrased instead of use your exact words. You might be tempted to begin again at step 1 in the communication process. Unfortunately, this is all too common an outcome. We tend to get wrapped up in semantics and expectations of a particular word or phrase instead of looking for the intent. This is the situation I call *heated agreement*. You are both arguing for the same thing, but because of a focus on the words rather than on the intent, people become flustered, thinking that they are not being understood.

After some time working together you will begin to develop a pattern. If your standard outcome is the first possible outcome, you might develop a trust from which you no longer expect your team member to repeat back to you. If your standard outcome is the second scenario, then your team member might truly appreciate the opportunity to get clarification on assignments before time and resources are spent. After a while, you will find that the second scenario will slowly progress to the first scenario after you have learned each other's style and values.

If your typical outcome is the third scenario, then it is time for an attitude check. Are you focused more on the words than on their meanings? You might ask another team member with whom you communicate better to facilitate discussions. Allow this person to tell you if you are being too literal or demanding of certain words or phrases.

With a self-imposed attitude check, or a third-party assist, you are less likely to enter a downward spiral of tension and frustration. Otherwise, you may begin to treat your teammate as if they are not a valuable team member, and they are likely to have an aversion to meetings with you. This is clearly an unsustainable situation.

Any of these three scenarios would be better than some situations I have been in. At one time, I had a boss who purposely would withhold his expectations because he wanted to see if we would "figure it out on your own." To him, these were simple tests to see how sharp his staff was. To his staff, he was a terrible and tyrannical manager for making his team waste valuable time and effort instead of just being up front with what he wanted. He also had a set and predetermined answer that was the only one he would accept. Anything different his staff came up with was never a viable solution. As this pattern continued, he became less and less effective as a manager and leader. He could have used an attitude check to determine if what he was doing was helping or hindering the team.

In my experience as a leader, working with a full-time employee was much easier when it came to developing a relationship and a comfortable communication rhythm than it was with volunteer staff. It may be because of the sheer volume of hours we spent together as opposed to the talent level. Having more time together each week allowed us to go through the process faster.

Still, working with volunteers gave me the most appreciation for having clear expectations and buy-in. There were fewer opportunities for volunteers to check in and verify their progress. There were fewer opportunities for the volunteers to ask for clarifications when they had questions. There were more opportunities to go very far in the wrong direction.

The most typical example in Toastmasters that I encountered for this was the selection of area governors by the district governor. While the organization has clear, written expectations for minimum requirements of the role of area governor, the common problem was that the district governor, who appointed them, had expectations that exceeded the written requirements. This usually led to a lot of conflict, where the area governor might be performing to the level of the written job description but not to the level of the "intended" job description. The solution to this was simple, if the district governor prepared a revised job description that included all the additional requirements, but this was rarely done.

There is another critical component to communicating clear expectations and getting buy-in. That component is the flexibility of the leader assigning the task to accept a result that, while it meets all listed qualifications, is not exactly what the leader had envisioned. This flexibility begins with an attitude of being open to the possibilities. If you are beginning a process or project and you "know exactly how it should look when your team is done," then you are not open to the possibilities.

There were many times in my career when I asked someone to prepare a report or conduct a program, and the results met all the requirements I had listed, but did not do so in the way that I had intended. One example that comes to mind is that time when I asked someone to prepare a packet of information for me with various reports. I had not expected the report to be bound, because I wasn't sure what order I wanted to place the reports. When I got the reports, they were bound, with a report order I had not approved, and I hated the cover design. Unfortunately, there was no time to redo the reports. We used the reports that I was uncomfortable with, but I hid my discomfort from the client because it would not have been helpful to the team. In the end, while I hated the cover and would have put the reports in a different order, the client loved the presentation, and even commented on how much they liked the new cover. It was then that I learned one of my most critical lessons. Stop being a control freak! Because one of my team members took the time to add something from their own talent, it made the end product that much better. From that point, I began focusing more on the function than on the form. What do I need this product to do? How it looks, or whether or not it has additional features are areas where my team can make further contributions. By their efforts and additional contributions, they are also taking ownership of the product, which in turn delivers a better product.

In the words of one of my previous managers, Mike O'Byrne, "Trust is liberating." I had learned that by trusting my team to do their best, I could focus my attention on other tasks that were still my responsibility. The more I trusted my team, the more they felt empowered; and the more they felt empowered, the more they took ownership in the project. The more they took ownership, the more buy-in we had as a team. The more buy-in we had, the more passion they felt for the work. The more passion we had, the better the outcome. It was an exhilarating process because Mike embraced the attitude of trusting his team to do their best.

Sometimes, you can spark this process with just an idea and then let the team come up with all the details. Brian and Ian were playing pool one night after an association meeting. Brian, the senior leader in the organization, simply asked, "Wouldn't it be great to have a statewide pool tournament for our association?" When Ian agreed that it would be cool, Brian simply responded, "Great. Make it happen." There were no details conveyed. There was no agreement of expectations and buy-in. There was just an empowering statement followed by liberating trust. In the end, it was an incredibly successful event that won statewide awards.

The process to get to this award-winning event was a series of committee meetings to harness the creativity and talent of the team. Nowhere in the empowering statement of "make it happen" was the *how* to make it happen. In fact, neither Brian nor Ian knew how to make it happen that evening at the pool hall. It was the passion and excitement of the possibilities that was contagious for the rest of the committee, and together they explored the specifics of how to make it all work. The clear expectations and buy-in were developed as a team. The only challenge remaining was the management of the time to pull it all together.

The success in managing the timing was accomplished in the setting of the deadlines and the schedule to complete the task. This aspect of the process had many moving parts and required careful coordination to make everything a success. It seems to be a natural law of the universe that the time needed to complete a task expands to fill the time available, even when the task is simple. In fact, Cyril Northcote Parkinson expressed this in what is now called "Parkinson's law." Give someone two weeks to do a one-day task, and what will happen? Most likely, the person will wait more than a week to begin the task because they feel there is ample time. Thus another natural law of the universe is revealed. Tasks started in the last minute cannot be completed in only one minute.

The first key to success in meeting the deadline is allowing your team member to set their own deadline. When do they think they can deliver the product to you? By allowing them to set the deadline themselves, they are taking ownership of the process and the product. You also know that they gave at least a little consideration to how long it will take to complete the project. When possible, accept the deadline set by your team member so that you leave intact his or her ownership of the due date. Employ the attitude that your team members can take some ownership.

There have been many times when one of my associates asked for more time than was available. One time in particular, I was working on a project in Santiago, Chile, and my engineering team needed a couple of months to complete an assignment they had just received. In fact, it was customary for the team to have up to two months to complete their work. The problem was that we needed their work completed before we could complete our task, which was due to the client in just six weeks; and we needed at least a week after receiving the engineering piece to complete the product for submittal to the client. Given all the parameters, I could not accept their original due date request, but I explained the situation clearly, in my best Spanglish, and we negotiated a mutually disagreeable due date. I say disagreeable due date because while we both agreed to the date, neither of us were happy with the amount of time available. Still, we knew that neither of us could extend the due date, and neither of us were the reason for the lack of time left available. We agreed to work together and be the heroes of the project.

A major component of our agreement was to set the follow-up time frames. Rather than just set a due date and then I sit back and hope that all ended well, we set up weekly check-in times that provided me the opportunity to see that progress was being made, and it gave my teammates the opportunity to ask questions at set intervals. Even though they knew they could contact me at any time with questions, it was beneficial to them to know that we would be meeting and that I expected them to ask any questions. I could tell how much progress was being made or not being made by the questions asked in these meetings. Very basic questions meant they were still in the beginning stages and had not made much progress. More intricate questions let me know that they were making good progress and giving the project a lot of thought. No questions usually meant that they had not started the project, which might result in my asking for additional follow-up meetings.

Let's go back to our natural law of the universe that tasks started at the last minute take more than a minute to complete. For some reason, the minute that is most often chosen to start is at the end of the work day when the product is due the next morning. This means that all of those questions that should have been coming all along need to be asked when no one is around to answer them. This can be avoided by having frequent follow-up times planned. Hold your team to their responsibility of delivering a quality product in the time set.

The best way to ensure success for your project or product is to make sure that you and your team members are clear on what is expected and what features the final outcome needs to ensure. Have a valid deadline, and have regular follow-up appointments so that you can keep each other on track.

- ✓ Are you prepared for misunderstandings to happen?
- ✓ Are you focused more on words than on their meanings?
- ✓ Are you helping or hindering your team?
- ✓ Are you open to the possibilities?
- ✓ Do you trust your team to do their best?
- ✓ Can your team members take ownership?

WHAT GETS REWARDED GETS REPEATED (PEOPLE WILL WORK FOR PEANUTS)

"Remember, man does not live on bread alone; sometimes he needs a little buttering up."

— John C. Maxwell

What motivates you to do a job well? Are you looking for recognition? Financial incentives? Respect? All of these are rewards. Though some are more tangible than others, all have the capacity to motivate a person or a team.

It is a simple concept, but one that often eludes the leader looking to maximize production from the team. Think about this: Whom have you worked the hardest for? Was it Boss A, who repeatedly told you that you were doing a great job and gave you a commendation? Was it Boss B, who rewarded other employees with commendations, making you wish you had one yourself? Or was it Boss C, who demanded you weren't doing enough and screamed at you until you produced more?

While Boss C may get more in the short run, the employee will burn out quickly and leave. Short-term gain is long-term loss. Bosses A and B both prove the benefit of "what gets rewarded gets repeated." One reward can motivate many employees. The employee who receives the award is now motivated to do it again and get rewarded again, but the employees who did not get the reward are also now motivated because they know the rewards are out there. This process is enhanced when a certain attitude is in place. That is, look for opportunities to reward instead of reprimand.

This is one of the ways in which leaders sabotage their own efforts without realizing that they are doing so. I once asked Boss C why he was so reluctant to praise a job well done. His answer was interesting. He said, "I don't want to overdo the praise because when you overdo the praise it becomes meaningless. By reserving my praise for only the best of jobs, it means more when I give it." He was correct that by giving it less frequently it had more impact on the team, but he should have reversed his logic.

By giving praise often we create the environment that our team always feels appreciated and empowered. In this environment, you reserve the negative reinforcements for worst of times when you can't let something go without addressing it. By using this approach, when you have to be stern with your team, it stands out more and they will take notice without you having to escalate the punitive measures to still get effect.

Consider it this way. When you freely give praise and empowerment and you find yourself in the situation to be stern, your team member will most likely say, "That was out of character. I must have crossed a line." When you are Boss C, who is always stern and find yourself in the situation to give praise, your team member will most likely say, "That was out of character. I guess they're not *all* bad." Which reaction would you rather have?

Does the reward need to be something lavish or expensive? No. In fact, it can be candy, a certificate, or something that costs just pennies to present. The idea is to make it something both suitable to the situation, have some value to the recipient, and, most of all, be something fun.

When devising your rewards program, you have to consider first what behavior you are trying to foster. Don't make it too many behaviors rolled into one program; try to keep it more focused. With that focus, it should be easier to identify the goal of the incentive. If you do ___, then you will receive ____. A good guideline is that if you cannot explain your entire incentive program in three short sentences, then it is too complicated. Keep narrowing the focus of the program until it can be explained easily.

So many times, we try to come up with a new and better incentive program than one that might already be working. In our efforts to reinvent the wheel, we sometimes reinvent the flat tire. If something is working, incentive programs are not often the place to be inventive because we are already having the effect on behavior that we are looking for. That is not to say that incentive programs that are working cannot be modified; rather, we should not redefine them too broadly. For example, we might change a successful program because it has become too easy for people to achieve, and we want our program to include stretch goals. We might set the achievement bar higher while still keeping all other aspects in the program intact. A program that required a 60 percent achievement before might now require a 70 percent or 80 percent achievement.

Another key to remember in creating incentive programs is to harness what already exists elsewhere. For example, in Toastmasters International, there is a Distinguished Club Program that has ten measurable goals. This program measures four aspects of club performance and has three levels of achievement and reward. It is a very complex program that many members do not fully understand. Those members who do understand it have been taught through various training sessions. This program is designed to drive behaviors in the management of clubs, and the program runs each year from July 1 to June 30. Universally, there are members who obtain and/or submit achievements within the last few weeks of the program, thereby meeting the programs goals at the last possible minute. In my local district, we decided we wanted to drive the behavior to have people complete their objectives earlier, so we came up with a program that simply said that if you achieved the minimum level of the program by April 30, then you would receive additional bonuses. This was well within three simple sentences, and since enough people understood the primary recognition program, it was easy enough to convey. Ironically, it also caused some who did not understand the Distinguished Club Program to learn about it so that they could obtain our bonuses.

The challenge for our team with this program was to determine what the awards would be. Certificates are nice when it goes along with something else, but not much of an award on their own. We decided to do vouchers for our bookstore because these rewards would essentially be used for educational products that would continue to help the clubs and members develop. Now we had to determine how much to award, considering that between one hundred and two hundred clubs could earn the reward. Some wanted to do $100 per club because they wanted to shock and awe with the cash value. Others wanted to do just $20 per club because they were worried about the sustainability of the program. You cannot continue to run the program if you empty the bank account on the first time. In the end, we decided on $50 per club with three additional prizes. The additional prizes were $50, $75, and $100 and were based on a simple drawing. Each club that achieved a Distinguished status two months before the program deadline would receive the $50 voucher and would be included in a draw for an additional prize. We had a program that was simple, sustainable, and provided the wow factor of big money without us having to worry about how many clubs would earn the reward. In the first year, it was moderately successful; but in the second and following years, it was incredibly successful.

On the whole, incentives where many people can achieve will be much more effective than those where only one person can win. Keeping the reward simple, yet fun, will allow you to provide the same reward to many people. In fact, the more inexpensive your reward is, the more sustainable the program becomes. Programs are always more effective after they have been in place a while and people know better how it works and what to expect.

It is always better to have rewards for measured accomplishments where many can be rewarded because this is better than rewarding just the single top performer. This uses an attitude of wanting to reward as many people as possible. People can often control what they produce, but they cannot control what others produce. The more you can keep an incentive program within the control of the person doing the work, the more chance for success there is. Imagine a reward program in which realtors from all over the country will be rewarded for total dollars of houses sold. A realtor in Manhattan sells one property for $2 million, while a realtor in Memphis sells nine houses for $200,000 each. The realtor who did less work wins because he happened to be in a more expensive market.

Rewards of this type that provide an advantage to one area or department over another will discourage teams in the disadvantaged areas from even trying, thus you receive little to no benefit in the areas that perhaps need the most help and encouragement.

The idea is to provide a reward structure that is not too much of a stretch goal because you want a lot of people to earn your reward. If you set the stretch goal too high, many team members will simply choose to not even try. Your incentives should get everyone excited about the possibilities and rewards ahead. Asking your team to produce an additional 20 percent is much more likely to get results than asking for an additional 50 percent. More people see the 20 percent as realistic and will try versus the few hard-core team members who will try for the 50 percent anyway. Even if they fall short of the goal of 20 percent increase, they may have had a 15 percent increase and that's still improvement. The attitude is really just to keep the incentive program simple, measurable, and fun.

While I was a lieutenant governor of marketing for Toastmasters, I learned of someone else who used M&M candies as a membership reward. I decided to give it a try and declared that M&Ms now stood for membership and marketing. At each event I attended, I asked people to stand up if they had helped a new club form or if they had helped to save a faltering club. Everyone who stood was thrown a pack of M&Ms. Yes, they were thrown from across the room. This actually made the presentation more fun. Everyone in the room was having fun and excited about the rewards being given so freely. I then asked anyone who had recruited a new member to join to stand and threw M&Ms to them. Each of these goals was a low bar to meet. Recruit one new member, or help to start one new club, or work to save one failing club. With the exception of recruiting a member, I wasn't even asking for successful results. I was looking for people who made the effort.

After each event, there would be people asking me for M&Ms because they didn't get any. I would ask if they had done any of the three things that got rewarded. When they admitted they had not, I would tell them that if they did, then the next time I saw them, they would get rewarded. I had people calling me and e-mailing me to tell me when they had done something to be rewarded and reminding me to bring my M&Ms to the next event they would be attending.

That year, our marketing goals were met earlier and with less stress than in previous years. The following year, my successor continued the tradition and saw even better results as our members knew more what to expect. Our marketing goals were met even earlier. The third year of this incentive program, the lieutenant governor for marketing discontinued the program. Our marketing goals were met, but it was a challenge to meet them in time. The year after that, the marketing goals were not met at all. This was proof that people would be happy to work for peanuts—especially when coated in chocolate and a colorful candy shell.

During the years that we used the M&M program, if someone stood at a subsequent event to get another pack of M&Ms for no more effort than had been done the first time, I was happy to give them the extra candies. This was because I soon came to realize that the energy and excitement that this generated was far more valuable than the mere pennies it took to purchase the candy. That is because the value of the reward was not in the price but in how it communicated to the recipients on the emotional level. Also, because those who had not yet done any of the three required tasks for the reward still saw someone else being rewarded. That in turn motivated them. It also illustrated that the rewards were plentiful and always enough to go around. It would have dampened the fun and energy for me to not provide the extra candies.

One thing to be careful of is a reward where you pick just one team member out of many, such as an Employee of the Month. The caution here is that someone who works very hard but never gets picked will eventually stop working as hard because they will become discouraged by the lack of recognition. Once an employee feels unappreciated, they will slow down production, look for another position elsewhere, or both. If you had a team of two hundred people, it would take you more than sixteen years to reward each person on your team using an of-the-month reward system. How long would you be willing to wait for your recognition? One way to provide a greater range of recognition using an of-the-month system is to let people know that they have been nominated. Think of any of the televised awards shows where our favorite stars and performers get those coveted awards. Just being nominated is an honor, and those nominations being made public is recognition enough. Add that component to your own of-the-month program and see if your overall production doesn't go up.

What gets rewarded really does get repeated, and that goes with both positive and negative behaviors. I worked for a company that had a particular report that measured performance factors. This is a concept from the Earned Value Management System in which you compare your *spent performance* against your *earned performance*, meaning that the number of hours or amount of money spent to complete a task was compared to the amount of earnings that you could claim credit for. This report drove behavior, and not always the behavior we wanted. Our team members found that they could claim more earnings by working on tasks only up to 90 percent and then moving on to the next task. You may not have realized that the last 10 percent of any activity takes a lot longer to do the detailed work and get something truly complete. If you are painting a wall, the time you spend with a roller in the middle gets a lot done quickly, where the careful work around the edges and trim takes a long time. That concept is fairly universal with many tasks.

Our report was intended to measure sustained performance, and we praised those with good rates while we interrogated those with poor rates. There were no candies, certificates, or cash prizes. Only the motivation of being praised or being questioned on why performance was low was enough. What we did not anticipate on this report was that our teams would not complete tasks on time because we were not measuring completion; we were measuring sustained performance. Our teams had learned that by not completing a task and moving on to the next, they could actually increase their sustained performance rates. In solving one problem, we created another.

- ✓ Are you looking for opportunities to reward or reprimand?
- ✓ Do you want to reward as many people as possible?
- ✓ Are you keeping programs simple, measurable, and fun?

PASSING THE PRAISE

> "Show me a manager who ignores the power of praise, and I will show you a lousy manager. Praise is infinitely more productive than punishment."
>
> —Michael Abrashoff, *It's Your Ship*

While some of the concept of recognizing team members is very similar to our previous chapter on working for peanuts, there are some differences that we can explore. These differences deal less with a formal recognition program and more with day-to-day interactions.

For example, as much as I tried to tell my assistant that she was doing a great job, she seemed to act as if it was just lip service. She didn't trust that I was giving her credit to the bosses for a job well done because she never saw me do it. My assistant was not in the meetings when I said that she had come up with a new approach to doing things on the project. My assistant was not in the department manager's office when I was singing her praises. In short, all of my efforts to pass the praise were not effective because perhaps the most important person did not hear them. I needed to keep the attitude in mind that the most important person to see the praise is the person being praised.

I eventually came to understand that I needed to make the effort to commend her on a job well done when she was there to see me sing her praises to others. I also came to understand that it was not me personally that she didn't trust but the specter of so many bosses before me who had actually claimed credit for her innovations and extra effort. It was easy for me to understand because I had been there myself. I had been in meetings where someone had taken credit for my work and done it right in front of me. If someone can be that brazen to do it in front of the person who really did the work, how often does this happen other times?

It is for this reason that we need to go out of our way to pass the praise. We need to look for opportunities to praise our team members when they and others are present. Staff meetings are a great opportunity for this. The simple mention of jobs well done during a staff meeting can yield so much. Your staff will feel much more valued and will be more motivated to add value back into your organization. All you have to do is keep the attitude to make your people feel valued.

This is also where Employee of the Month programs can really have the desired effect. As discussed in the previous chapter, imagine how effective the program would be if you did not just announce the recipient of the award but everyone who had been nominated as well. Then even though they may not have been selected because someone else had a more outstanding contribution that month, they can still feel recognized in public.

I once worked on a project where the department manager held a monthly staff meeting. He would mention each employee who had been nominated for Employee of the Month and what they had done to be nominated. After all the nominees and their accomplishments had been mentioned, he would present the winner with a large bag of licorice candy. Even though the candy was not expensive, it was fun, and other employees at the end of the meeting would surround the recipient and share the candy. The amazing result was that instead of employees feeling imposed upon for having to share the prize, they actually enjoyed sharing as they received accolades from more team members.

Some companies have instituted on-the-spot recognition programs, where any member of the staff can give an award to any other member. These awards may range from simple thank-you notes generated by a web-based recognition system, to low-dollar-amount gift cards to local merchants. Depending on the contribution, and management approval, some of these awards can be bonuses of $1,000 to $2,000. What makes these programs successful is the incorporation of three points. The first is that any team member can initiate the recognition. This could be because some managers are not always aware of the team member's value to another team member, or because some managers are just not good at recognizing team members either in public or private.

I worked with Dawn for many years, and Dawn would help conduct large-scale training sessions. She would show up a day before the instructors and ensure that all logistics were in place, and she would stay late after the training to wrap everything up and ship everything back to the office. Despite her dedication to the course and her time away from her family, the department management sometimes forgot to recognize her efforts. In fact, they would often leave her to pack up while they would go on to other activities, which was extremely demoralizing for her. When I had the chance to conduct a course with Dawn in Brisbane, Australia, I helped her pack up and then took her to dinner. It was Dawn's birthday, and she was half a world away from her family, so I took her out for an expensive dinner. That type of recognition meant so much to Dawn, and my immediate supervisor was thrilled that I was watching out for our other team members.

The second point of the spot rewards is that the rewards are public. Everyone can see not only who is given an award but who gives it. Because awards can be generated by any team member, this creates an environment where your team members begin to think about who they can nominate for an award just to keep the fun going. Instead of recognition being reserved only for managerial levels, it creates an opportunity for everyone to get involved.

The third point that makes programs such as this successful is that the reward is immediate. One of the cardinal rules in training animals is that both positive and negative reinforcements must be immediate, or else an association between the event and the response cannot be made. While we are certainly smarter than the animals we train, the concept remains that rewards made immediately will have a stronger association between the act and the reward increasing the likelihood of repeated performance. People are always more responsive to rewards when they can remember what they did that was extraordinary to deserve the commendation. This is one reason that yearly bonuses don't often have the sustained effect over a full year. Instead, the desired behaviors are observed more immediately following the bonus and again immediately preceding the time of bonus formulation. The best way to sustain year-round performance is to sustain year-round recognition.

As a side note on annual bonuses: You should be aware of what your team considers substantial versus what you consider as substantial. I had the opportunity to observe the bonus disbursement for a company of roughly sixty employees. Only fifteen of those employees would receive bonuses, but that was the tradition there, so no one objected to this practice. In one particular year, the company saw record profits, and when they calculated an algorithm to see how much employees should share in the profits, the result was close to $300,000 to be shared. When the CEO announced the bonus pool as $40,000, the CFO was upset because he knew that the CEO was keeping the additional $260,000. The highest bonus paid to any one employee was $5,000, while most received $2,000. The staff were all happy with their bonuses because it was the amount that they had always received, and because they were not aware that they were almost the recipients of a substantial windfall. The point of this example is that while the CEO could have paid out much larger sums that year, he was probably wise to pay out normal sums. This is because the annual bonuses happened sometime after the changes in behavior that changed revenue had been put in place, but also because the bonus program remained sustainable instead of necessitating the setting of new expectations. Though this CEO did not implement a spot recognition program, it would have been a great use of some of that extra $260,000 that would have produced much more return for the company in the end.

Your team members are like cars. They show up on their first day with a full tank of gas and that fresh, new-car smell. As their leader, you can drive them to accomplish a great many things. You can get them to stretch and strive for heights greater than they ever believed they could reach, at least until they run out of gas. Your team members need constant refueling to continue to run properly. It's a simple attitude that the more often you refuel their gas tank, the higher their productivity becomes. How would your car run if you refueled it only once in a year?

There are many ways to refuel your team's gas tanks all year long. Some of them are a wise investment in your organization's development, while others cost little to no money. Some ways to fill the gas tank that are a wise investments are team appreciation lunches or dinners, spot-reward gift certificates, and company merchandise. Some ways to fill the gas tanks that cost little to no money are to recognize birthdays of team members at monthly team events, pot luck lunches or dinners, and casual days if your office is normally held to a dress code.

On one project I worked on for five years, we worked in an office space with our client. This created an atmosphere where we were always under the spotlights and had little room for error. Our client worked a schedule where they observed every US federal holiday while we observed only eight standard US holidays each year. This meant that several times each year, we were required to report to work on days that our client was off. These days were casual days, meaning we didn't have to come to work in office attire, and we used to hold a miniature golf competition during our lunch break where eighteen small fairways and holes were set up around the office. This made the day fun and energetic rather than employees feeling somehow robbed of a day off. This did not cost the company anything, but the team gas tanks were all filled, and the benefits were beyond measure.

- ✓ The most important person to see the praise is the person being praised.
- ✓ Do you make your team members feel valued?
- ✓ Are you looking for ways to refuel their gas tanks?

DEALING WITH NONPERFORMERS

"A competent leader can get efficient service from poor troops, while on the contrary an incapable leader can demoralize the best of troops."

—Gen. John "Black Jack" Pershing

It is just a fact of life that someone on your team, whether you selected them or they were assigned to you, will be a nonperformer. This may be because they are simply not capable of performing to the level required, or it may be an issue of time management, or it may even simply be an issue of motivation. Your first course of action needs to be identifying not just the problem but also the underlying reason for the problem.

The most difficult position we find ourselves facing is the situation in which someone has oversold their qualifications for an opening on our team. This difficulty is amplified after you have invested considerable time and money into training this person, only to find that they do not have the required skill set to perform the job. In this case, I recommend you take a long, hard look at their attitude. Do they possess enough of your core values that they may be useful somewhere else in your organization? If so, you might still come out ahead in this scenario if you maintain the attitude that it's best to salvage what you can.

One possible solution is to simply limit their workload until they can develop the skills needed to do the job they were hired for. It is likely that their roles and responsibilities have many facets and the work can be divided into multiple parts. Perhaps some parts can be given to other team members in the interim, or perhaps some of the roles and responsibilities can simply not be dealt with for some time. This forces us to determine exactly what roles and responsibilities are mission critical and which are the proverbial icing on the cake. Adopting an attitude that you can make their job easier could possibly make the difference between developing a team member instead of losing a team member.

There was one team member I worked with who had his own ideas for how he was going to accomplish his responsibilities. When he shared his planned methodologies with me, I was greatly concerned that he would not accomplish the work in the amount of time available. Wanting to be the encouraging leader, I shared my concerns and let him make his own decisions on how to proceed. A few months later, my concerns were becoming a reality, and we were falling behind on our goals, which included revenue generation. As I counseled him on how to improve his performance, it became clear to me that he was unable to handle all the aspects of his role. I reassigned some of his duties to other team members and assumed some of his responsibilities myself. At the end of this division of efforts, he still retained the title, and he still retained about one-third of his original workload. It was still a challenge to keep him focused on his remaining one third because he still wanted to be involved in those roles and responsibilities that were now being handed by others. After some time, he began to make significant progress on his remaining goals, and gradually, we were able to start reassigning roles and responsibilities to him. Though not all of his roles were reassigned to him, the overall effort was still successful in both accomplishing the goals of the organization and in developing our team member to be more capable.

On another project that I worked on, the person who assumed the lead role was someone we pulled out from a similar role in another project. When senior management asked me if I felt this person was capable of doing the job, I responded with a simple question. Was there someone else in our organization who could be assigned to that role instead? I knew before I asked the question what the answer would be—that we did not have a deep enough bench in that remote part of the world. Our only option was to keep this person in the lead role but make the extra effort to mentor him and train him to become the team member we needed him to be in the first place. It took several months, but eventually, this person began to demonstrate the skills that we needed to harness. It was a challenge at times, but our commitment to this person's development paid off in the end. To do this, we had to keep an attitude that our most important role was to provide support and resources to help this person develop.

There will be some times that you can retain a team member that you have already invested in, and you can use them in a way that makes them more productive. Though they may not be a great fit for the role into which they were hired, there may be another role that plays to their strengths. This may mean a demotion in some cases, but often, a team member would rather remain on the team than be removed completely.

There was on instance on a major construction project when we brought someone in to lead one of our teams. Mack came well recommended by another of our project managers. Unfortunately, Mack did not work out on this new project because his skill sets were more suited to maintaining a project that was already set up. We needed someone who could set up a project. Mack also did not possess the leadership skills we had hoped for. We needed him to lead the team, but he was averse to taking on a leadership role, even though that was part of the job requirement. The manager responsible for staff assignments was pretty upset and chose to reassign him to another project that required a setup. This project needed two people, and the other person assigned to the project was also someone who did not perform well on another project. This was like tying two stones together, hoping they would help each other float. It would have been better to assign each of these people to a project with a strong leader who could mentor and train the staff to make them stronger team members. In the end, Mack was demoted to another role where he could maintain an existing project rather than rely on skills he did not possess. He was happy to be in a less stressful situation while still being of value to the organization.

There may be times where the person brought in for a job does not possess the required skills and is not committed to developing those skills either. In these cases, they need to be reassigned to a lesser role, or they need to be invited to join a different team where the skill sets they have can be useful. Keeping someone around who is not contributing can be detrimental to the rest of the team in terms of both production and morale. This is perhaps one of the most difficult attitude checks—being able to determine when it's time to stop working to salvage. An old expression goes that the best part of hitting your head against the wall is stopping. When you stop doing something that was clearly not going to be productive, there is an immense sense of relief in having made the decision to move on.

There was one assistant I hired who had been with his previous firm for seventeen years. His references glowed:

he was a great team member, and I was eager to have him start on my team. George started, and I gave him a lot of responsibilities right away. However, I soon found myself staying late many nights correcting his work. I made many attempts to help George improve his work product, but I quickly came to realize that his seventeen years of experience was really one year of experience repeated seventeen times. He simply did not have the capabilities I needed to get the job done, and more importantly, he did not have an interest in growing into the role. While he and I were having many meetings to discuss how he could improve his work product, he was already interviewing for other positions with other companies. To be honest, I was relieved that George removed himself from the situation rather than push me to the point of firing him. Once he had left, I was able to fill the position with a better candidate, and our project benefited greatly from the change in team members.

One important aspect to note in my experience with George is that my own leadership capabilities were not as developed then as they are today. It is entirely possible that had I known about these attitude checks earlier in my career we might have had a different outcome. My style then was much more along the lines of the command and control model and it was years later than I began to see the benefits of the reward and responsibility model.

Another component to keep in mind is that for some of your team members, being able to utilize the command and control model can come in handy. If you have a member of your team who was in the military for many years and is not performing, being able to draw on their experiences in the military might provide the motivation they need to reach deep within themselves and ignite that flame that makes all things possible. If you are unable or unwilling to employ this model, it might help to pair this person with someone who was also in the military and can harness those shared experiences and emotions. A simple yet powerful example of this is when I go for a run I often wear something that says USMC. I have been out of the Marine Corps for more than twenty years, but if I am wearing something that says USMC I cannot give up too easily. I won't let myself give up while wearing this gear. I have spoken to other veterans who do the same thing.

If the issue is one of time management, it would be helpful to make resources available to the team member so that they can learn better time management techniques. Of course, part of this analysis needs to examine what they do spend most of their time doing. You might discover that they are always busy but do not have enough hours in each day to complete an entire task. Often, the function that suffers most in this situation is the quality control, meaning that the person has just enough time to perform the task but does not have the time to check their work for errors.

You might also find in this review that the tasks that your team member is spending the most time performing are tasks that are not mission critical but, rather, are the tasks that give your team member the most enjoyment. This could be a great opportunity for you if you can find a team member who loves to do tasks that other team members try to avoid. It might be possible to have the team member who loves the task perform this task for everyone, and similarly, the tasks that this team member does not enjoy might be performed by the rest of the group who now have more free time in this deal.

The one situation we hope we never find ourselves in is the scenario where our team member is simply not motivated to do the work. In today's environment of Internet distractions like social media and web surfing, this becomes even more common. The best way to handle this is to help the team member come to terms with their motivation issues and have them decide if they want to be a productive part of the team or if they would prefer to move on. Perhaps there is an opportunity to help them with time management skills so that they can do their social media or web surfing at a more appropriate time. It is more likely, however, that their motivation issues stem from something else, such as poor leadership. If they have not been recognized for their work, rewarded for their efforts, or made to feel a valued part of the team, then they begin to seek enjoyment elsewhere since they are not getting the enjoyment from their work. The best way to get these people to engage again is to give them the recognition they were missing in the first place.

- ✓ Are you trying to salvage what you can?
- ✓ Can you make their job easier?
- ✓ Your most important role is to provide support.
- ✓ Sometimes it's time to stop.

DEALING WITH CONFLICT

"At the root of every tantrum and power struggle
are unmet needs."

—Marshall Rosenberg

Conflict happens. That is surely not a surprise to you, but the real question is, how do you manage it within a team where it may not just be conflict between you and one other person but could be conflict between two of your subordinates or two of your peers? There are many different ways that conflict can manifest, and even more ways to deal with it.

There are many books dedicated to this subject alone, so clearly, this book will not solve all your problems in a single chapter; but let's see if we can give you some of the basic solutions to help you through most situations.

We often use the expression "Let it roll off like water from a duck's back." It's better to remember that we are not birds, and that means that you don't have feathers to get ruffled. Don't take things so personally that you let what is probably an honest misunderstanding get in the way of getting the job done. When something does happen that ruffles your feathers, it's time for an attitude check. Take a good look at yourself to see why it bothers you; and more importantly, ask yourself how you can learn from this for the future. It may be that this person has overstepped some boundaries, but it is just as likely that your boundaries were in the way of where they were stepping. As I have often told my team members, you cannot step on my toes if they are not in your way. This is an open invitation to my team members to step up and participate rather than feel they must refrain from contributing to a better outcome. By maintaining the attitude of encouraging participation, we have fewer drawn-out conflicts as everyone is contributing to possible solutions.

When something does happen where a team member has overstepped his or her responsibilities, we need to deal with those situations. Rather than get upset, work on resolving it so that it doesn't happen again. You can't change what already happened.

There was a team of new Toastmasters Club Officers I was mentoring in South America. Though the roles were clearly defined, one of the team members took it upon himself to receive a request from another organization and pass it along to the membership without first clearing it with the other members of the executive committee. This was a clear case of a team member overstepping his bounds because it was not his decision to make and also because the membership should never be informed of something prior to that information being shared with the leadership team. We took that opportunity to put in place some simple agreements and procedures. The first was that no decision would be made by only one officer, even if that decision was in the defined roles and responsibilities of that officer. The second was that no information would be provided to the membership without first briefing the club president. These were simple rules that most club officers would have known, except that these officers were the first officers in this area and did not have a lot of previous examples to follow. As they began to learn their roles better, we were able to refine the processes.

One highly critical thing to remember is to not make it personal. People can have disagreements, but once it becomes personal, there is no limit to the lengths that someone will go to in order to hurt the other. Do your best to not take things personally. The right attitude to have is to trust that your teammate is focused on business, not personal, issues. Even if the conflict is personal, use an attitude check to find a way to make it impersonal.

How do we make the conflict impersonal? It's best to start with an acknowledgment that the conflict seems to have become personal. You might even find ways to compliment the person to make them less defensive. From there, see if there is some common ground on which you can agree and try to move forward from there. Once you have found some common ground, and are working together to get to a solution, then you can begin to reinforce the fact that your conflict should not be personal. Try not to lead with the expression "This isn't personal, it's just business." That expression is too trite to be taken at face value.

In moving forward with these resolutions, we strive to make sure the issue is not personal, but the communication must be highly personal. Reach out to your teammate face-to-face or over the phone, because in either form of communication, your voice inflections can play a big part to convey sincerity, and therefore calm the situation. E-mail is a dangerous choice for these types of communication because the recipient will read the e-mail in the tone they are feeling at the time. If they are feeling hostile, they will interpret your e-mail to contain hostile intent.

Keep in mind that no one wants to fail, and no one wants the worst possible outcome. If that is true, then you both want what is best, but you differ in your idea of how to get there. Even if you have competing interests, people are more apt to look for the win-win options when the situation is not personal. Begin with an attitude that everyone wants the best outcome, and look for the common ground for a starting point in discussions.

In one conflict I was involved in, we had not only the conflict between us, but it had been exacerbated by other people fabricating stories and spreading rumors. We had been competing for the same promotion for a year, which is stressful enough, but the rumors and the involvement of others just made the situation untenable. Though we made many efforts to keep things on a professional level, they nevertheless became personal. The more personal it became, the more vicious the rumors got, and there was widespread damage to many working relationships. After the selection for the promotion, the situation went from personal to emotional. Other people in the organization had become so vested in the outcome that they too took it personally that the person they supported was not promoted. This was a simple case of runaway attitude. Both of us needed to remember that our original goal was to serve the organization rather than ourselves. We needed to correct our attitudes to remember that it was not all about us but, rather, the organization.

If you are dealing with conflict between two of your team members, and you are in a situation that hinges on this conflict to be resolved, it helps to start with the understanding that you alone are not apt to bring about the magical resolution. No matter how insightful you might be, and how sage the advice you have to offer, your team members are more likely to play you against the other person in an effort to gain validation than they are to take your guidance.

When dealing with team members, the best approach is to get them speaking to each other instead of through you as the intermediary. It might help to give them some incentive to resolve their issues. That incentive might be some reward for resolving the conflict, or the incentive might be some penalty for failing to do so. The important part is not the incentive but the fact that you remove yourself from the middle of the conflict. This is not to say that you should not get involved. Rather, once you have set the stage for your team members to resolve their conflict themselves, you should step back and let them work through their issues. Any resolution between your team members is more likely to be successful if they arrive at it themselves.

Early in my career, I was involved in a dispute with another coworker. To this day, I don't know why we didn't get along, but we didn't. Eventually, our manager called us both into his office and gave us an ultimatum. Either we resolved the issue between us, or he would fire both of us. It was short and to the point, and more importantly, it worked. My coworker and I never had another disagreement. We still didn't get along, but we each had a reason to not let our issues detract from the project. In essence, we weren't pulling against each other, because we had found a neutral gear. Sometimes neutral works well enough to allow people to do their jobs. Not finding that neutral gear most likely means that one or both people will continue to sabotage each other's effort, either through inefficiency or interference. Sometimes we need to adjust our attitudes so that instead of trying to force two competing sides to agree, we just need to find a neutral gear so that hostilities can stop.

Later in my career, I had two assistants who were constantly asking me to settle disputes between them. One would come to me and complain about the other. Then the other would do the same. After many one-on-one conversations with each of them, and many meetings with both of them, I was still unable to help them resolve their issues. I remember what had worked so well for me many years before. I called them into a conference room and told them both that they needed to resolve the issues between them, or I would fire them both and start over. It worked in that they resolved their issues quickly and without my further involvement. However, looking back, I think I could have pushed myself to find a more respectful approach to arrive at the same conclusion.

Often, our leadership journey is about learning lessons and using retrospection to look back at how things went to analyze how they could have been done differently. Because we have a tendency to dissect projects that did not go well, we will learn more from those projects than from those that went well. This is also because when a project goes well, we just congratulate ourselves and move on to the next without going over it to see why it was a success. Sometimes we also have the opportunity to learn from the mistakes of others instead of having to make them ourselves. One of the lessons I was able to learn from someone else was to value the intelligence of your team members and not presume that there are no other smart people around. My coworker helped me learn that the quickest way to turn a team against you is to act as if no one else is as smart as you.

I once worked on a renovation program where some tunneling work needed to be done. Designing the tunnels was a very long and intensive process. We hired a tunneling engineer to come in and lead the effort of completing the design work because much had already been done under a previous manager who was being promoted. Even though he had managers who were technically capable, and even though a lot of smart people had been working on this program for more than two years before his arrival, he began his first day on the job by telling everyone what needed to be done. He did not ask a single question about what had been done, and he did not consider that anything had been done correctly previous to his arrival. It is a simple realization and attitude check: smart people were there before you and will be there after you.

What he said went something like this: "You have to determine the alignment of the tunnel from point A to point B using no more than maximum grades and turning radius." What he should have said was, "What grade and turning radius did you use to determine the alignment?" By turning his command into a question, he would have in fact validated what the team had already done and perhaps learned early on that he was working with competent team members. Instead, he continued to speak in a condescending manner to his teammates, and he quickly alienated them. Needless to say, he did not last long on the program.

Another great example of this predisposition to conflict is when a new politician is elected to a governing body, or when a new board member comes into a board of directors with the agenda to "fix" the organization. This is not to say that some organizations don't need help in changing how business is done, but when someone comes in with such an agenda, they are putting everyone in a defensive posture from the beginning. By adopting an attitude of learning the role and building cooperation, the new leader or team member encourages a team to be more effective, making it easier for changes to come into fruition. In this attitude approach, you first observe to learn exactly how things are being done, not just the part of the process viewable to the public but also what happens behind closed doors. Once you have better learned how the organization functions, you are in a better position to find a cooperative approach to help things run more productively.

We can avoid a lot of conflict with some simple attitude checks. Are we making an issue personal when it does not need to be personal? Are we doing our best to deescalate a personal conflict and return to a professional environment? Are we helping our team members to resolve conflicts at the lowest possible level? Are you treating your team with respect?

✓ Why are your feathers ruffled?
✓ Are you encouraging participation?

- ✓ Trust that your teammate is not making it personal.
- ✓ Understand that everyone wants the best outcome.
- ✓ It's not all about you but the organization.
- ✓ Find a neutral gear so that hostilities can stop.
- ✓ Realize that smart people were there before you and will be there after you.
- ✓ Learn the role and build cooperation before making changes.

MAKING TOUGH DECISIONS

"It doesn't matter which side of the fence you get off
on sometimes. What matters most is getting off. You
cannot make progress without making decisions."

—Jim Rohn

Let's just agree now that some decisions are unpopular
no matter what the outcome. It may be a situation
where two competing interests are involved and one will
not like the outcome, such as whom to promote. It may be
a situation where no one will like the outcome, but it has to
be done, like raising your prices. No matter what the tough
decision is, there are a few guiding principles that should
be followed.

The first is to confirm that a decision must be made.
Indecision is not the key to flexibility, though sometimes
we put ourselves into a tough spot because we have
declared that a decision must be made when in fact the
situation could likely work out through a natural course of
events. Even when a decision must be made, some people
avoid making decisions because they are afraid of making
the wrong choice. Some people avoid making decisions
because they don't want anyone to be upset by the decision.
Some people have other reasons for suffering from "analysis

paralysis." If this is you, please just breathe, close your eyes, relax, and make a choice. Here are a few ideas to help you make the right choice.

1. Make a list of pros and cons. No, this is not a trade secret, but it is a helpful step anytime you have a tough choice to make.

2. Map out some likely outcomes, including possible unintended consequences.

3. Verify your likely outcomes and various options against your original needs and plans.

4. Make the best decision you can from the information available and be satisfied that you have done your best.

5. If you are still unsure, flip a coin. I realize that this sounds...well, flippant, but there is a reason to flip a coin. Check to see how you feel about or react to the outcome. If you see heads and realize that you were hoping for tails, then your decision should have been the tails option before you flipped the coin.

Before any decision is announced, an attitude check should be done to evaluate how much the decision affects you or others. Who is the beneficiary of the decision, and are there any unintended consequences? There are some decisions that are in our purview to make, but when we step back, we might realize that others are more affected by the outcome than we are. When these situations present themselves, this is an opportunity to allow your team, or those affected, greater input in the decision-making process.

When I was a district governor in Toastmasters International, my two lieutenant governors asked me to allow them to conduct a training session in a geographic region of our district that was under-served. After some quick consideration, I was confident that our role at the district level was to remain centrally focused on our resources because we had other levels of support who were tasked with supporting more remote areas. I was sure that once we held a training event at one remote location, other remote locations would begin to complain that fairness demanded they be provided with training events as well. Though I was against committing the resources needed to conduct a training session in such a remote area, I also recognized that I was not the person who was going to have to deal with the eventual fallout or unintended consequences. Upon realizing that my lieutenant governors would bear the brunt of any discontent, I advised them of my feelings and rationale but allowed them to make the decision. After they discussed it, they agreed to conduct the training in these outlying areas. Regardless of whether or not the events were successful, my team felt supported and empowered, and that was the success I was looking for.

This was one of the few decisions where I was not immediately impacted by the outcome in my role as district governor. In fact, most decisions impacted me to a greater degree than it impacted either of my lieutenant governors. Though we functioned as a trio, and I tried to let majority rule as much as possible, I also warned them early on that there would be times when they might both disagree with me, but I was still going to make the decision I felt was right based on my broader view of our obligations and based on my experience of having assumed each of their roles previously. I called this "pulling the district governor trigger" because I knew that going against both of them on one issue was a shot across the bow. I also used that term because of a previous issue that arose when I first assumed the role of district governor.

At the beginning of each administrative year in Toastmasters International, a district is required to submit a modified alignment plan to reflect any changes in the distribution of clubs across the support structure of the local district. Strict guidelines control how many clubs can be assigned to one area. It became necessary for me to suggest an alignment that I knew would be unpopular with some of the affected clubs. I informed them early of the proposed alignment change and asked for their input. If they could find an alternate alignment that would prevent the reassignment of some clubs, I was open to any and all suggestions. Several weeks passed, and I had heard no suggestions, though I had heard many complaints. I didn't want to start my term with this conflict, but I was unsure how to avoid it. I called a past leader whom I greatly admired and asked for his advice. He said, "You're the district governor. Sometimes you just have to pull the trigger and make the tough decisions. Then move on. They won't like it, but you have done everything you can to avoid the conflict."

He was right. I was content that I had done what I could. Then I pulled the trigger and didn't look back. It was a tough decision, but it was the right decision.

Here are a few more guiding principles that we should keep in mind. The first of these is that bad news does not get better with age. What do you hear whenever there is a scandal? What did they know, and when did they know it? It's better to get the news out there quickly so that people have time to adapt to it, and perhaps avoid some of its impact. It's also better to make the announcement with sufficient detail for people to understand the rationale. There are few reasons to keep people in the dark on why you made decisions. By making people aware of the rationale, they still may not agree with your choice, but at least they will feel more valued for having been informed.

When we don't provide a clear rationale behind our decision, the lack of information will leave people guessing at the reasons. In situations like this, very few people guess correctly. It is far easier to tell people the correct reasons with the first announcement than it was to spend the time defending against all the incorrect reasons that will be conjured up by the masses.

A special note about social media in making announcements of decisions: There are many people on social media who find their value in being the first with breaking news, or who want to give their personal spin or take on an issue. If your organization has an active social media network, you need to be sure to announce any decision first on social media, and then via other avenues, to the masses. With this announcement, you have the opportunity to set the stage for every issue. If you don't get ahead of the social media enthusiasts, you give your detractors the first opportunity to frame the debate, and you will spend much more time on the defensive.

- ✓ How much will this decision affect others?
- ✓ Who is the beneficiary of this decision?
- ✓ Are you prepared to pull the trigger?

OWN YOUR MISTAKES

"You're going to leave my island a whole lot smarter
or a whole lot stronger."
—Every Drill Instructor at
Marine Corps Recruit Depot, Parris Island, SC

No one is perfect. It's an expression that everyone has used at some point in time yet so few remember at the right points in time. This is important for both you and your team members because neither you nor any of your team members is perfect. In either case, a good leader must know how to deal with these situations with grace, tact, and poise.

As we got off the plane at Beaufort Air Station, the quote above was shouted by my Marine Corps Drill Instructor. We were at boot camp in Parris Island, South Carolina, and these words told me I was going to make mistakes. More importantly I was going to learn from them. I was going to either be smarter and stop making mistakes, or I was going to be stronger from all of the push ups. I am proud to say that I left Parris Island a little of each.

Don't be afraid of failure and adversity. Keep the attitude that you are going to embrace it and learn to value it. As I mentioned before, more lessons are learned from dissecting the failure than are learned from dissecting why something succeeded. More importantly, give yourself and your team members permission to make mistakes so that you can learn from them. Life is a learning laboratory, and experience is a wonderful tool to help us recognize a mistake when we have made it again. You cannot stop mistakes from happening, but you can make them a valuable part of your team environment.

I once took a series of classes on improvisation at the Hideout Theatre in Austin, Texas. One of the things the instructor had us do was literally celebrate every mistake. When one of us made a mistake, we would throw our hands upward and sound a triumphant scream to declare, "I failed." Immediately after, everyone else in the class would applaud and cheer to celebrate the failure with you. It felt weird and even awkward at first, and still it was an extremely liberating and refreshing experience. This was called the failure bow. I highly encourage you to do it sometime when you have made a mistake. Perhaps in the middle of your office cubicle farm is not the best place to try this, but try it sometime.

In too many environments, when we have made a mistake, we feel pressure to remain perfect in the eyes of our team. This protective attitude comes across in many forms and prompts many bad behaviors. Some will blame team members for giving bad information. On one project, we had a monthly meeting to review every project on our program with our client and representatives from other departments. I prepared the reports for the meeting based on updates from our project managers. I was surprised at how often project managers would report information that was vastly different than what was on the report. When they were asked why the information they were reporting was different, they would say that the report was wrong. This put me in the line of fire as people questioned my ability to produce the reports properly. Luckily for me, I had saved their handwritten notes, and in the next meeting, when they declared that information on the report was wrong, I showed them their notes. Suddenly, they were claiming that information had changed rather than declaring that the reports were wrong. Of course, much of this could have been avoided with an attitude of teamwork where we supported each other rather than with an every-person-for-himself approach.

In some situations, some people will claim that they did nothing wrong even in the face of evidence to the contrary. Pride becomes a more powerful force than anything else, and some people will stop at nothing to protect their pride. They apparently don't realize that there is great value in being seen by your team as human. It lets them know that you are not setting an impossible standard to follow or live up to. When you show your human capability to make mistakes and then own your mistakes, you develop a trust with your team. If you can own your mistakes, then you are less likely to attempt to blame your mistakes on their efforts. Another great benefit is that owning our mistakes relieves us from the pressure of having to make excuses. Those who make excuses too often will eventually lose credibility—not only with those they lead, but also with those they follow.

One of my most challenging lessons on owning one's mistakes was when I had a colleague, Megan, who had overstepped the bounds of her position and, as a consequence, the reputation of others was compromised. What Megan did was clearly inappropriate to everyone except her. She should not have been involved in the first place, but she was concerned for others who were involved. In her attempts to resolve one conflict, she created a larger problem. All anyone wanted from her was the acknowledgment that her actions were wrong and would not happen again. An apology would have been icing on the cake. What we got instead were staunch statements that she had done nothing wrong. As management continued to ask for acknowledgment that this would not happen again, Megan got more and more defiant that she had done nothing wrong. Eventually, other managers needed to become involved in what should have been a minor issue. What could have been over and done with in a matter of mere moments began to drag out instead, and the operations of the organization suffered as a result.

In examining this whole situation, it helps to remember that Megan never intended to cross any lines; nor did she intend to be inappropriate. In fact, she had a lot of love and passion for our company, so the last thing she wanted was to hurt the organization, but pride got in the way. The simple inability to accept that no one is perfect created an impermeable barrier to reason. In retrospect, Megan could have simply not agreed that her actions were inappropriate but still agreed to not repeat the behavior. This would have at least put a cap on the damage and allowed the team to move forward.

Because so many of the other managers who got involved agreed that she had overstepped her bounds, what Megan should have done was to acknowledge that with so many others convinced that what she did was wrong, perhaps there was a lesson to be learned. If we have done something that another finds objectionable, it is possible that that other person is just being oversensitive or perhaps are incorrect in their interpretation. When several others hold the same opinion that we have done something objectionable, we should take stock of the fact that many with differing perspectives have examined the same situation and arrived at a similar conclusion.

When others are sure that we have done something wrong, it is important to recognize that we may have done something we did not intend. When this happens, the best course is to apologize for having offended our teammates.

I have heard some people apologize by saying, "I'm sorry that you were offended by my comments," but that is not an apology. That is putting the blame on them for being offended. It is more appropriate to say, "I'm sorry that my comments offended you" and own that you did something you may not want to do again. When someone has been offended or otherwise damaged by our words or actions, it is important to find a quick remedy to avert further damage. Attempts to explain ourselves in an effort to convince the others that they are wrong typically aggravate the perceived injury. This has the same effect as digging a deeper hole in our effort to get out of the first hole we have dug. When you find yourself in the proverbial hole, stop digging. Adjust your attitude to one of learning when to apologize. Good apologies are a strong medicine.

Go the extra distance after apologizing for an inappropriate action by thanking the team for their patience and support. It is often the actions of going the extra distance that spells the difference between still-festering foul feelings and turning an otherwise embarrassing situation into a personal public relations victory. Even something simple can be a chance to put this into action. Jon Miller was a Vice President I worked for, and he was always extremely busy. If you were lucky enough to find him in his office, it was to see him with his nose to the proverbial grindstone. Even with so many demands on his time, he did a great job of demonstrating this when I showed up in his office doorway one day to go over some brief issues. Although he was busy with paperwork, he had also said that it was a good time for him to talk with me. As I talked, he continued working on his papers. Suddenly, he stopped himself and said, "I'm not giving you the attention you deserve." And he proceeded to focus on what I was saying. Something that simple really made the difference in how valued I felt and how I viewed Jon as a leader. His stock went way up in my book.

We've all grown up hearing that actions speak louder than words, but what does that mean for leadership? It means that when you convey through actions a message that contradicts what you have told your team, it can demoralize them quickly. Consider this question for a moment: Why should you be able to trust your team if they cannot trust you? If they cannot trust you to own your mistakes, then they are likely to posture in ways to protect themselves, which in turn diminishes how much you can trust them.

Preschoolers learn that the golden rule is to do unto others as you would like them to do unto you. As adults, we learn that the golden rule is that he who has the gold makes the rules. It is ironic how often the adult version of the golden rule leads to conflict, whereas the preschool version rarely does. Perhaps this is an opportunity for an attitude check to embrace the preschool version of the golden rule.

In his book, *Relationship Selling*, Jim Cathcart introduces a concept of the Platinum Rule. This is later developed into a full book titled *Platinum Rule* by Tony Alessandra. These gentlemen bring us to the concept of taking the preschool version of the golden rule a step further and encourage us to treat people as *they* want to be treated. In other words, find out what makes them tick and go from there. The brilliance in this concept is simple yet sometimes difficult to implement. We often do think to ourselves that we would be okay being treated one way only to find that we have inadvertently created a conflict. It takes an exceptional attitude to genuinely put someone else's needs and interests first, and that attitude almost never leads to conflict.

- ✓ Make mistakes and embrace them.
- ✓ Team members support each other.
- ✓ Good apologies are powerful medicine.
- ✓ Embrace the preschool version of the golden rule.
- ✓ Embrace the Platinum Rule

BROADCAST YOUR MESSAGE ON WIIFM

"You can have everything in life you want, if you will just help other people get what they want."

—Zig Ziglar

Even though we have our own goals to reach, we need to understand the most basic concept that people care more about what they want than what we want. It's normal. It's natural. It's just what we need to understand to accomplish our goals.

Consider going fishing for a moment. How many fish do you think you would catch with just the hook and no bait? You might get lucky, but you are certainly not setting yourself up for success. You have to put some bait on the hook, something to attract what you are trying to catch. I happen to be partial to steak and potatoes myself, but that won't work for most fish. Worms, on the other hand, are something that the fish seem to go for. I wouldn't eat a worm, but then again I am not trying to catch myself. I am trying to catch the fish and I have to use what appeals to the fish's taste and not my own taste.

As we begin to craft our message to our team, we need to perform an attitude check to consider what bait we are putting on the hook. Is this something that appeals to us or the team members? Are we driven by facts and figures? Is our team? Are we framing our message in a way to be sent, or are we crafting our message in a way to be received?

While serving as a district officer in Toastmasters, I often heard the accusation, "You district officers are only interested in the numbers. You don't care about the individual." Of course, this claim was completely incorrect, but it helped to highlight a critical misconception because of my miscommunication. As district officers, the only tools we had to evaluate our progress and efficacy were statistics and reports. The reports measured any number of metrics and accomplishments. The reports were categorized into levels of organizational leadership so that people serving at various levels could immediately see information and progress against their own set of goals. The reports were how we judged ourselves.

Since these reports were what we had learned to monitor, the numbers were what we focused on and, thus, what we reported on when we asked our members to help us achieve the district goals. We were missing the most critical point of all: no one else cared as much as we did about the district goals. It's not that they didn't care about our desire to do well. It's not that they didn't care about the program. It's that these were our goals and not theirs. We were not looking for ways to represent the goals in terms of why it was important for each and every member. In short, we were not broadcasting our message on the station WIIFM (What's in It for Me?)

We needed an attitude check to reduce the accusations of us being only about the numbers. We needed first to ask ourselves why our information would matter to other members. Of course it mattered to us, but would any other person find that information of value? Would any other person be inspired to work toward these goals? After discovering these perspectives, I stopped reporting accomplishments or goals in terms of district-level goals. I would still print them in my monthly progress reports, but I never spoke about them in my update presentations. Instead, I broke the numbers into smaller levels of leadership that were being measured. If I was reporting to division level leaders, I reported that their numbers needed to reach their own goals. If I was reporting to area-level leaders, I reported their numbers to reach their own goals. Suddenly, I was not promoting my goals. I was talking to them about reaching their own goals. This was another attitude check. My role as a leader was to help them achieve their goals. Instead of them helping me reach my goals, I was helping them reach their goals. This had a tremendous effect, in that not only did it help them to focus on their own efforts, it also helped them to feel supported instead of driven. There is an old adage in politics that the voters don't care how much you know until they know how much you care. Helping your team members understand that you care is a key component to broadcasting in WIIFM.

In almost every organization, there are various levels that require someone to perform basic management and supervision. There will be a set of goals for the entire organization that have been set forth. While some organizations are adept at breaking those goals down into smaller goals based on the lower levels of management, most organizations do not go down to the individual team member. The individual team member is where all performance happens. Departments and divisions do not accomplish anything without a committed team of individuals making things happen. The key in motivation is to motivate people at a personal level. Your attitude must be focused on the mission that you have to give them a reason to care. The best way to do this is to harness their own goals and objectives.

In many volunteer organizations, people join the organization to achieve specific goals. Those goals rarely include the recruitment of new members, yet that is one of the first things we as leaders in this volunteer organization ask them to do. Those goals rarely include pursuit of various other goals within the organization, yet that is also what we push them to do because we may have quotas we are trying to meet. Too often, from the moment the new member joins, we focus on how they can help us meet our goals rather than focusing on how we can help them meet theirs. We lose sight of the fact that the organization goals are usually a roll-up of the individual goals.

In business, the converse is often the case. Individual or department goals are often the breakdown of organizational goals. For a company, a vision is set to increase sales or productivity, or perhaps to earn some industry recognition.

I have seen so many companies where they advertise a new campaign to increase sales or production by 80 percent. Banners are hung from the walls, and maybe even some T-shirts are printed to commemorate the event. The problem is that there is no WIIFM component. Why should the employees care if sales increase by 80 percent? If they work on commission, then clearly there is a direct benefit; but if they don't, then you are asking them to work 80 percent harder to fill someone else's pockets. Does that sound motivating to you? If it does, then I would love to have you work to increase sales of this book by 80 percent and thank you in advance for your help. You can see it as a joke here in this book, but too many companies do this with serious intent.

I was working on a project in Texas, where the senior project management staff had brought up the issue of how difficult it was to correct work that had been installed poorly. Many times, the poor installation didn't fail or become a significant problem until after the workers had gone home and the warranty period had begun. This is the period of time that most workers will never know about any issues or problems, so why does it matter to them if the company has to go back and fix something?

After an impassioned plea from the senior managers to take the time to do the work right and not create these warranty situations, it was clear that the workers were still not aware of why this mattered to them. They were concerned only with finishing one job and moving on to the next. It was then that I added to the conversation that I had just finished working on a proposal where the prospective client was requiring bidders to list similar projects they had done, complete with a list of all warranty issues. I explained that our company's ability to get new work was dependent on them doing good work. More to the point, their ability to have longevity with our company and work for one company for twenty to thirty years was dependent on the quality of their work. That was a personal message that let everyone know that our ability to keep them employed was within their direct control. It was the same message, but broadcast on WIIFM.

- ✓ Are you crafting your message to be sent or received?
- ✓ Are you focused on something that matters to others?
- ✓ Are you helping others achieve their goals?
- ✓ Have you shown them how much you care?
- ✓ Have you given them a reason to care?

MAKING UP FOR LOST PRODUCTION

"Lost wealth may be replaced by industry, lost knowledge by study, lost health by temperance or medicine; but lost time is gone forever."

—Samuel Smiles

You can't turn back the clocks, and you can't move the deadline. Now what do you do to still make the target completion? The most obvious answers are to add more resources or to work the people you have for longer hours. Let's look at each of those options and see which is best for different situations.

Too many times when we are behind in our production or our goals, the tendency is to add more supervision to push the work harder. People seem to feel that just adding enough extra managers will somehow get the wagon moving again. In fact, this often yields the opposite result while increasing your costs. Instead of having a positive impact, there are now more managers making more demands for reports or meetings that the execution team is now further distracted. If the managers had an attitude of find the problem then find a solution, this would be a wonderful benefit to any team. Unfortunately, the attitude is often one of *knowing* what the problem is already and acting on that presumed knowledge.

Common Problem:
Stuck in the mud and cannot proceed

Obvious Solution

All too common solution

When additional resources can be assigned, there needs to be a clear path forward in using these additional resources so that they, too, do not become wasted or stuck. Even if additional resources are readily available, you need to first determine if the problem is a matter of resource availability or of execution strategy. Sometimes, the resources you have are enough to get the job done if you just refine your strategy.

I was working on a project in South America where we were under pressure to produce a very complex project schedule. We had a team of five planners working on the project already, but time was short. One of the managers on the project decided he was going to ask for more resources to get the job done, even if the additional manpower needed to be pulled off of other projects. What this manager had not considered was, what were these additional planners going to do? This one question seems so simple but can often be the toughest to answer. The answer must come in the form of a division of responsibilities. In fact, the project was under pressure because the original team was not well organized in terms of division of responsibilities, so adding more people to this already-chaotic situation would not have improved the outcome. Furthermore, pulling those resources from other projects would have hurt those projects.

Before we made the request to bring in additional resources, we made a detailed list of the work that remained to be done. We then assigned team members to each item on the list. When we were done, we found that we already had enough people to get the job done and didn't need to bring in any additional resources. Now that the existing team had a better understanding of their responsibilities, they were better able to get the work done within the time available.

Many times, this is the case. Existing resources can accomplish the tasks at hand if they are better directed. There are also times, however, when making the detailed list of work to be done reveals that there is simply too much work for the existing team to accomplish. In these situations, you will need to bring in additional resources. The key is that when bringing in additional resources, you can be clear in what they are expected to do and how long the task should take.

Sometimes there are no additional resources available, and we must extend the hours of our current resources. This can be done by adding the number of work days or the number of hours worked each day. For example, if someone is already working five days per week, we might increase that to six or seven days per week. Or if someone is working eight hours per day, we might extend that to nine or ten hours per day. Before making any changes, you must first do an attitude check to ensure that you are aware of how valuable your team's time is to them. It should be equally valuable to you. Recognizing that your team's time is valuable is paramount to showing appreciation for the extra efforts and sacrifices.

Whether we extend the hours each day or the number of days, we need to recognize that our team members need some downtime to recharge. Working our team too many hours and/or too many consecutive days will lead to burnout, and productivity will actually be worse than if we had done nothing different. Each of these has benefits and drawbacks, so let's take a look at each option; but before we do, we will do another attitude check. Are you aware of how much your team needs time away from the tasks at hand? Work-life balance is crucial to healthy relationships both in and out of the workplace, so before adding time to the schedule, weigh the need against the impact.

If we add whole days to the work schedule, that provides a great block of time in which to be productive. So much can be accomplished in this environment, and your team may appreciate the opportunity to clear some backlog. If your staff earns overtime pay, then they might really be thankful for the chance to earn some extra money. If your staff does not earn overtime pay, whether they are salaried or volunteers, it is often helpful to provide some additional reward for the extra hours. Perhaps providing meals or some other tangible benefit that they don't normally get will help ease the fact that they are giving up the time they would otherwise use for family activities, running errands, or simply for downtime to relax and decompress.

Perhaps the biggest drawback of adding whole workdays is that it accelerates the time frame in which your team burns out. People need downtime to rest and recharge. Adding whole days, even if the work hours are shorter than normal, is perceived by the team to be an entire day lost.

One way to avoid this rapid burnout is to add an hour or two per day. Since people are already at work, it is often easier to just keep them a bit longer. Just a few hours each day also means that it takes longer for your team to reach the burnout point. The drawback is that you have less time in blocks for productive work, and it can cause issues at home if someone is needed to pick kids up from daycare or be home to prepare dinner.

A significant challenge to getting your team on board with the effort is to properly motivate them to participate. You might remember the scene near the end of *Animal House* when Bluto shouts, "What? Over? Did you say 'over'? Nothing is over until we decide it is! Was it over when the Germans bombed Pearl Harbor? Hell no!" After more attempts to rally his troops, he yells, "Who's with me?!" and goes running from the room only to find he is alone and he returns to the room deflated.

Sometimes we feel like this when we are trying to convince our teams to work harder or longer hours to make up this lost productivity. The key is to remember to be appreciative of their efforts to date. Remember that the extra time you want them to give up is valuable to them. It's not about you or what you would be willing to do. It's about them, and we already established that you need them much more than they need you.

I once had the chance to mentor a coworker, Kenan, who continued to demand his team to work additional hours. He was not asking his team to do any more than he was doing himself, so he felt completely justified in making the continued demands. Kenan could not understand why so many of his team members were requesting transfers to other projects, and some even gave ultimatums that if they could not be transferred, they would quit. In fact, these transfer requests made Kenan even surer that his team was being unreasonable. What Kenan was missing, however, was that his team needed to be respected for their additional contributions. They had families at home who were complaining of not seeing them enough, so they not only had conflict at work, they also had conflict at home. When faced with this continuous conflict, work will rarely win in the end. My advice to Kenan was to start asking his team to put in the extra hours instead of demanding that they put in the hours. This simple act showed respect for the team and helped them to feel valued rather than taken for granted. The other thing I suggested Kenan do was to take his team, and their spouses, out to dinner. Part of this suggestion was to specifically thank the spouses for their sacrifice. Showing this type of appreciation helps limit the amount of conflict at home and relieves a lot of stress for your team members. After all, why create conflict when you can alleviate it?

If you work in a deadline-driven environment, it is important to keep deadlines achievable so that your team is not always in recovery mode. Additionally, if your deadline is far enough in the future, you can work additional days for a month, then an extra hour each day for a month, and then back to normal hours. This three-month cycle done twice will recover a lot of time and avoid the burnout issues.

For one project I worked, the managers had a habit of committing to client deliverables to be available the first workday after a long holiday weekend. The managers thought they were doing the team a favor by slipping in the extra few days to get the deliverable ready. What they were really doing was ensuring that their team would never have the long holiday weekend to recover from the overtime and stress. To further the insult to the staff, they never got to enjoy the holidays that the rest of the teams were off for. Not only was this team burnt out, but now they were envious of other staff members who had been assigned to different projects. It would have been much better for the team to work hard and then rest with their families and friends.

A couple quick notes about burnout: First is that as people grow more tired, the productivity drops, and over time, it could drop to less than simply working normal hours. Another consideration is the type of work, because as people become more tired, then safety can be at risk. This is why flight crews and commercial drivers are required to have a specified amount of rest between shifts. Lastly, the more burnt out your team becomes, the more they begin to call in sick or just not show up at all. Absenteeism is a sign of burnout, and it can also be a sign of other issues, such as ineffective leadership.

- ✓ Remember that their time is valuable.
- ✓ Remember that they need time away.
- ✓ Don't create conflict if you can alleviate it.

GROOMING YOUR SUCCESSOR

"Before you are a leader, success is all about growing yourself. When you become a leader, success is all about growing others."

—Jack Welch

Even the thought of grooming your successor has to begin with an attitude check. If you are not replaceable, then you are not promotable. If our goal is to be promoted, then we should begin looking for our replacement as soon as possible. Grooming your successor actually provides three specific benefits.

The first benefit is that you demonstrate your leadership skills to your upper management by letting them see how you are with your team. If your team performs well, then that reflects upon you as a leader.

Don't be surprised if the person you are grooming to be your successor doesn't trust that your intention is to build them up. It is not uncommon that people have had negative experiences in the workplace more than they have had positive experiences. I once had an assistant, Emily, whom I had hired because of her senior technical skills and because I wanted her to become my eventual successor. I told her on numerous occasions that my plan was for her to take my position when it was time for me to be promoted; but her experiences with previous supervisors had been negative, so she didn't trust my intentions. Because she was not in all the same meetings, she did not witness that I always gave her credit for her work. More importantly, because she did not have full access to all of our client staff, she thought I was holding her back.

What was really at play was that in our client organization, there were two project managers who had a history of demanding that some of our team members be removed from the project. Once someone on the client team makes that request, there is no recourse for us to keep that team member on the project. From time to time, we can keep them in the company and assign them to another project; but my goal with Emily was to keep her on the project to become my successor. Because of my time on the project, I had earned the clout with those project managers, and even with the management levels above them. It was because of this clout that I decided to keep those demanding clients on my division of responsibilities, and I had Emily work with other project managers.

The time did come that I was transferred to another department when an opportunity opened up, and Emily took over my role. She did a great job in the role because she had been given most of the responsibilities of the job before she had the title. When she took over the role, she also had the clout needed to withstand any criticism of those two client project managers who were known for "voting people off the island." After she had been in the role for a while, she came to realize that I had been in her corner the whole time.

The second benefit is that you actually improve your own understanding of the role and of the leadership issues when you teach someone else to do your job. Having the attitude that you are willing to train and mentor is needed to do this. Teaching forces you to break down the process to basic components and communicate them to someone else. Additionally, having someone ask you challenging questions forces you to search for answers that you may have not considered before. Teaching and mentoring helps us solidify concepts that we intuitively knew by making them more tangible.

The old adage is that "those who can, do, and those who can't, teach." That may be true for some physical tasks where people who can no longer engage in the physical aspects become coaches or teachers, but for any task, those who teach enjoy the process of a more profound level of learning.

Even though I had been in my profession for more than twenty years, and I had been in many different technical and leadership roles, my understanding of my own profession deepened greatly once I began training newer staff to fill this role on their projects. These were concepts that I was completely comfortable using, and yet I began to understand them in ways I had never considered. Mentoring and training others is not only crucial for the development of future leaders, it is also imperative for our own development.

The third benefit is that while you are waiting to be promoted, you have someone who is capable of filling your role to make it easier for you to divide the work into more manageable portions and also to fill in for you when you want to take a vacation.

It might be comforting to think that your job security is not an issue because your company or organization can't function without you for even a couple of days, but that also means that you do not get the downtime that comes with a real vacation that is uninterrupted by cell phones and e-mails demanding your time and attention when you are trying to relax. Just as it is important for your team to have downtime to decompress and avoid burnout, it is important for you to have downtime to decompress and avoid burnout.

Grooming your successor will free more of your time so that you can have a balanced life and so that you can have time to continue your own development. Leadership is not an exclusive club where the seats are limited. Leadership is an open family where there is always room for one more. By holding development and opportunity close to the vest, you are treating leadership as the exclusive club. This is your final attitude check. It is the summation of so many of the other attitude checks because from here, you must be prepared to move forward yourself into a new role, and you must let someone else continue what you started. Many times, leaders cannot sit back and watch someone else take the reins. Sometimes people feel as if they need to get actively involved to ensure that things continue on the right course. This is called meddling. True leaders don't meddle once they have moved on because if you have done a good job at training your successor, then you don't need to meddle.

Are you opening yourself to the possibilities that exist when you mentor, train, and groom the next generation of leaders to take your place?

- ✓ If you are not replaceable, then you are not promotable!
- ✓ Are you willing to train and mentor?
- ✓ Are you willing to let go of the reins?

Remember that most problems in leadership occur because of our attitudes, and most can be solved by changing our attitudes. Therefore, it is important that you check your attitude early, check your attitude often, and, most importantly, check your attitude at the door.

Heath Suddleson LIVE

As a speaker at major events, conferences, and internal business meetings, Heath Suddleson shares information critical to organizations on three critical topics.

The Attitude Check: Lessons in Leadership has been tailored to fit into keynote speeches, educational seminars, and coaching points for individual consultations.

"Get Up To Speak Without Needing An Ambulance Before, During, or After Your Presentation" is an informative session in which Heath shares key strategies for overcoming the fear of doing presentations while building your confidence to become an effective and persuasive speaker.

"The Keys to Effective Feedback" is a presentation that shares proven techniques to better give and receive effective feedback. This will enhance the workflow and camaraderie in your organization the minute you start using these techniques. Don't just use them in the office. Try them at home. They are not only for trained professionals.

Heath is a dynamic and powerful speaker who has earned acclaim for combining a professional stage presence with a poignant sense of humor to help audiences gain critical skills while enjoying themselves in the process.

If you would like information on having Heath visit your organization, or if you would like to order some of his audio and video resources, please call or visit:

+1 (301) 538-9158 or (888) 923-4618
Fax (888) 923-4619
www.executiveachievement.com
www.attitudecheckthebook.com